W0019726

logbook

hiromi suzuki

first published by Hesterglock Press
The Blue Room
25 Wathen Road
Bristol
BS6 5BY
UK

www.hesterglockpress.wordpress.com

ISBN 978-1-9999153-1-5

copyright © hiromi suzuki 2018

The right of hiromi suzuki to be identified as the author of this work has been asserted by her in accordance with the Copyrights, Designs and Patents Act of 1988. All rights reserved.

Art director / Design : Paul Hawkins and ichigo yamamoto

Contents

You won't believe it, everything is useful . . . even this pebble for instance	1
The backside of the moon shines the light of day	2
Have you ever walked on the coast of the moon?	3
m for mortal	4
e for embrace	5
water flow, water fall	6
wellspring	7
the forsaken chronicle 1	8
the forsaken chronicle 2	9
Mascarets	10
M.D.	11
Where troubles melt like lemon drops	12
That's where you'll find me	13
cross-talk / off-line	15
Trouville en automne	17
Waiting For The Ship "Night"	19
from the fogged window	21
about logbook	23
Mare Vaporum	39
Post It	50
The seasons	57
(Untitled)	70
Burger Burglar	76
artist statement	83
acknowledgements	84
artist bio	85

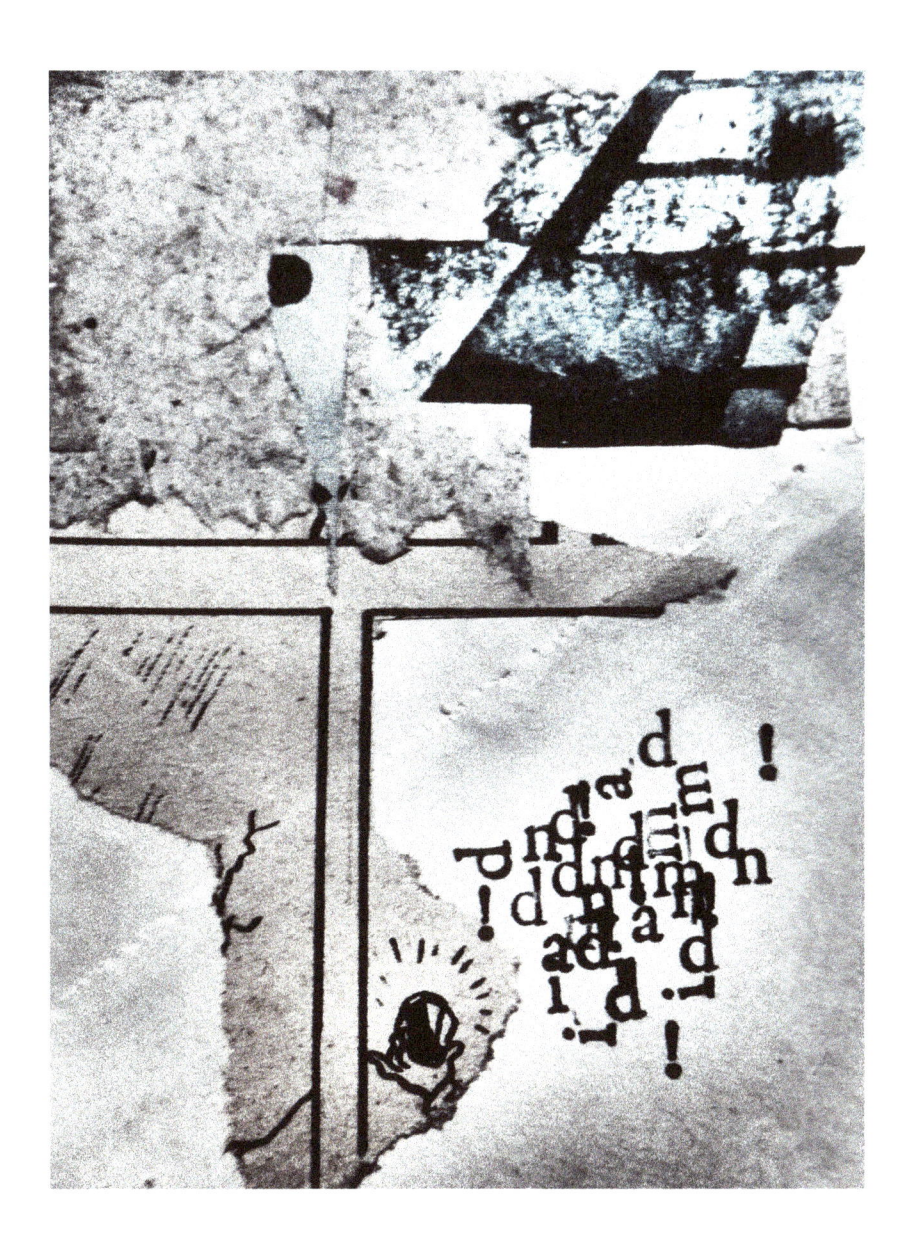

You won't believe it, everything is useful . . .
this pebble for
instance

The backside of the moon shines the light of day

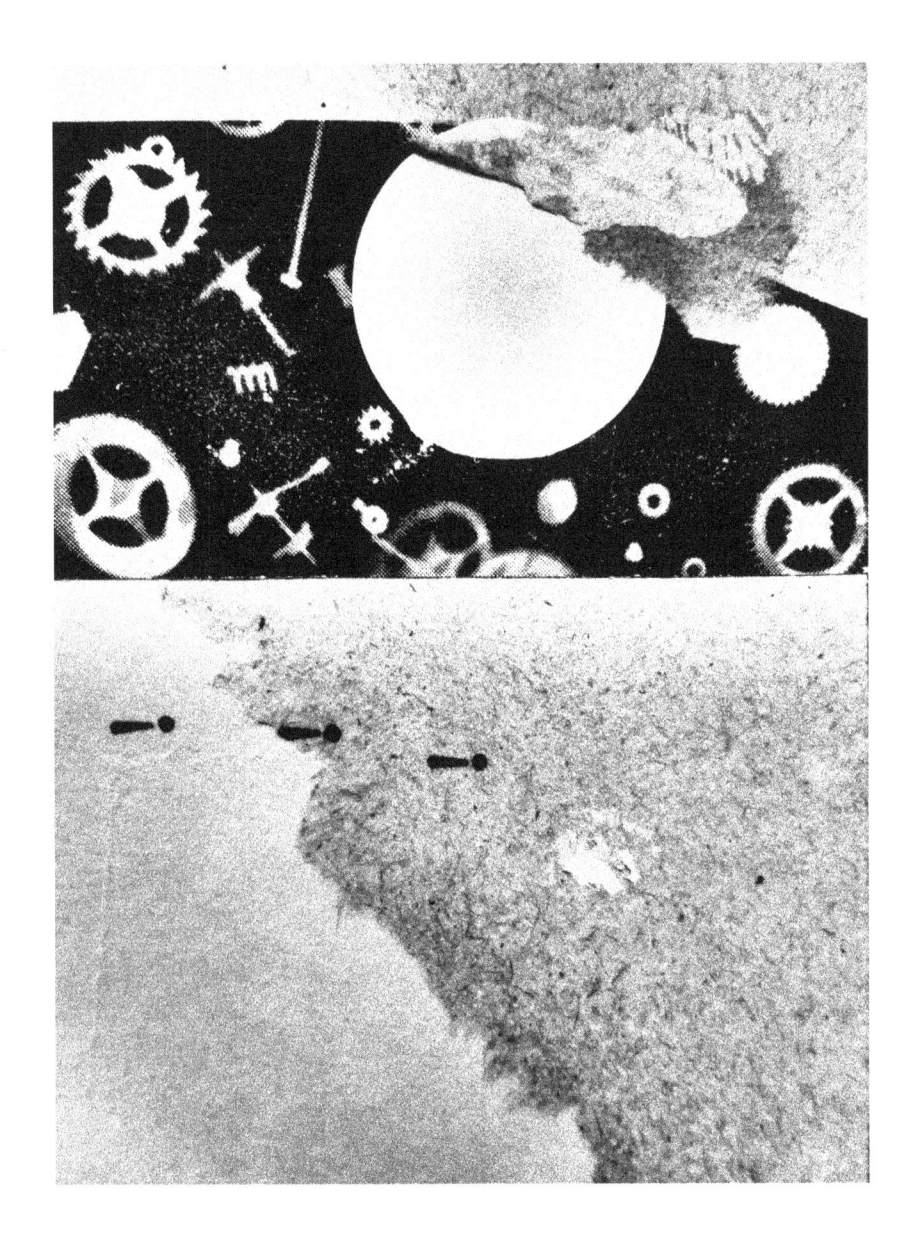

Have you ever walked on the coast of the moon?

m for mortal

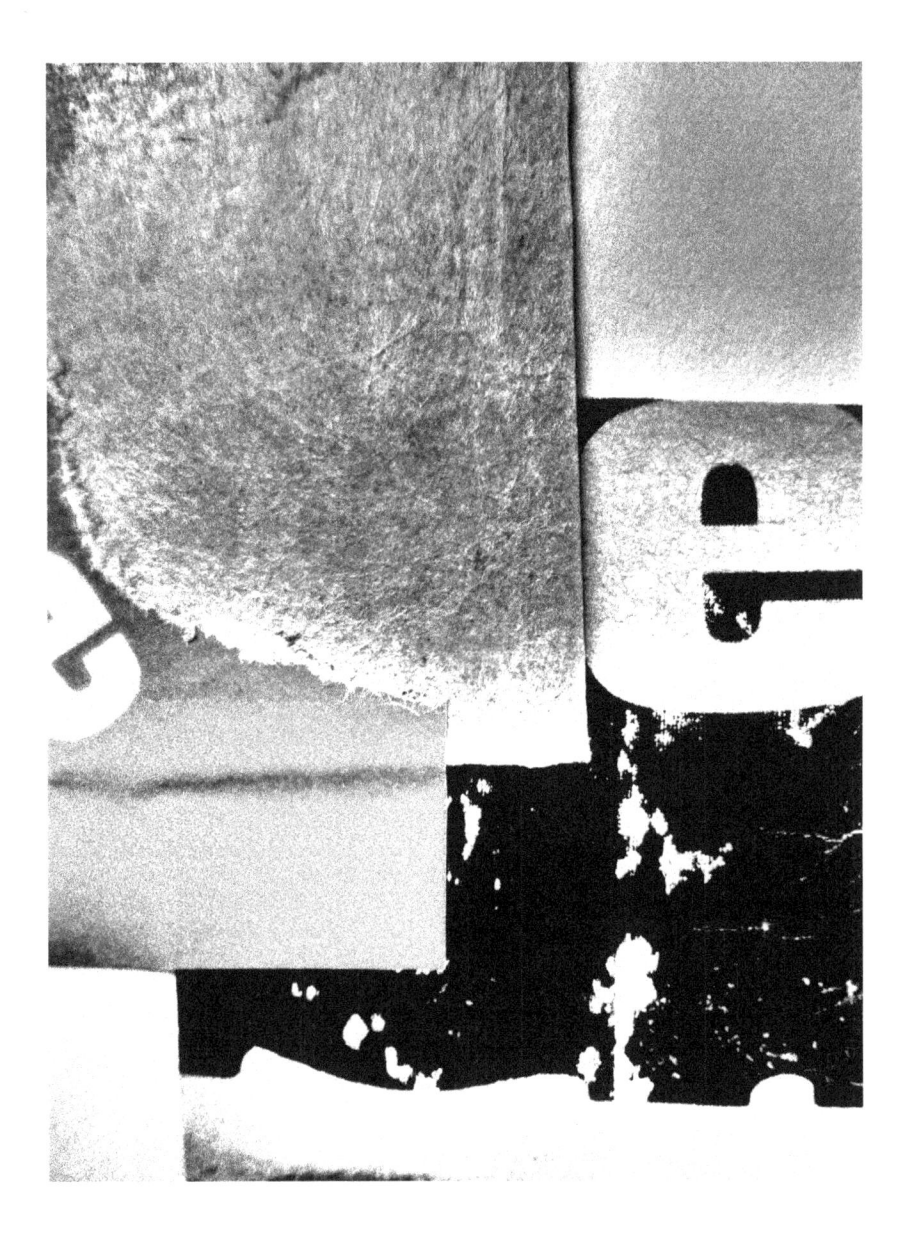

e for embrace

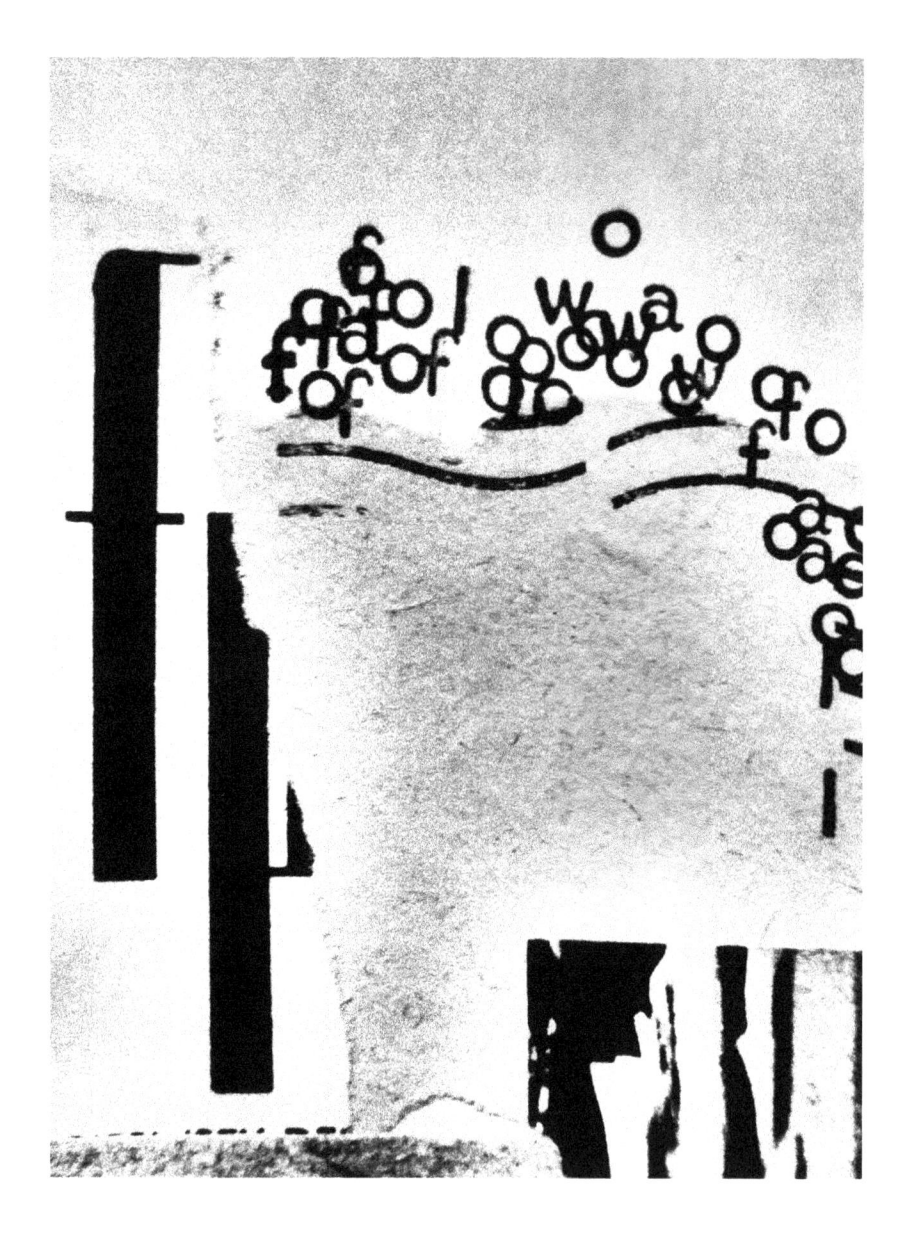

water flow, water fall

wellspring

prima che ho e po
il risult generalm
concorsi afferma
ni, sarebb di posti
vene insie Allora
più diffic lavoro da
comincia co lo spunt
quali i due coniugi so
mars su quelli dove
determinata. Il più de
che l'uno dei coniugi
l'altro, affermando ch
bello ma lui, oppure

The forsaken chronicles

Mascarets

M.D. *inspired by "M.D." (Yann Andréa, 1983)

Where troubles melt like lemon drops

That's where you'll find me

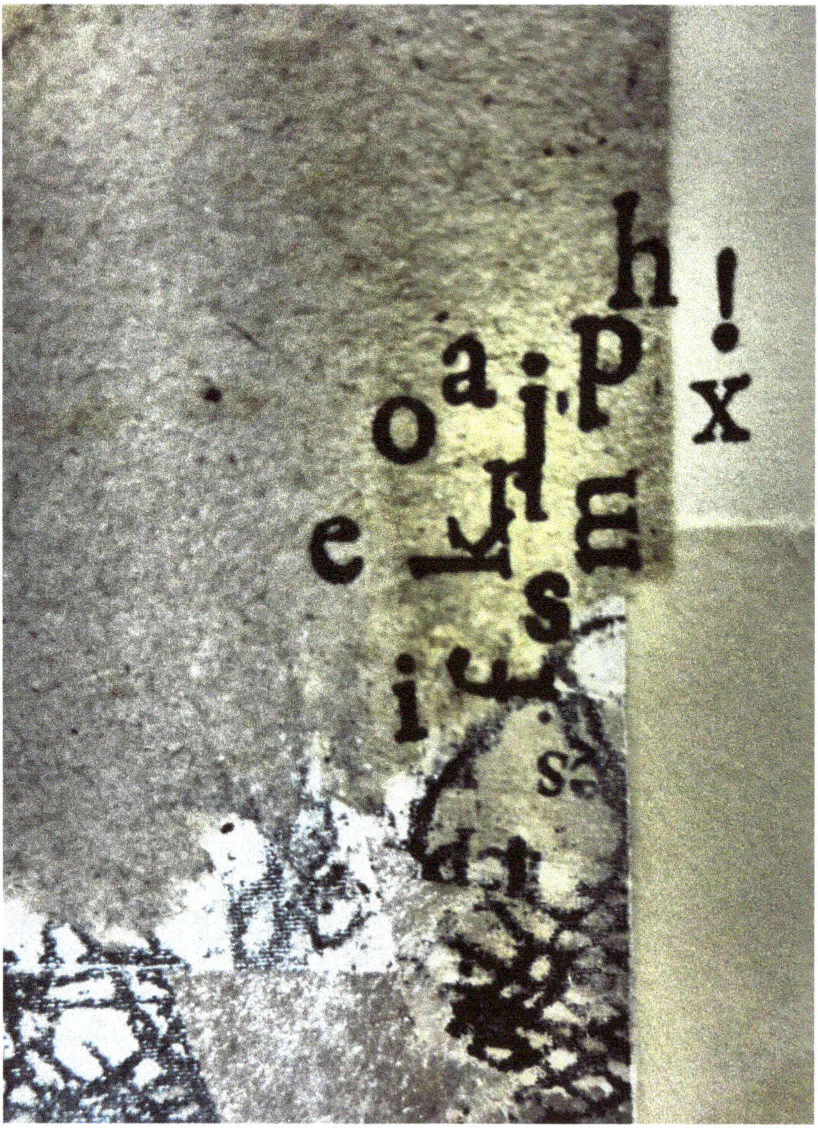

cross-talk / off-line

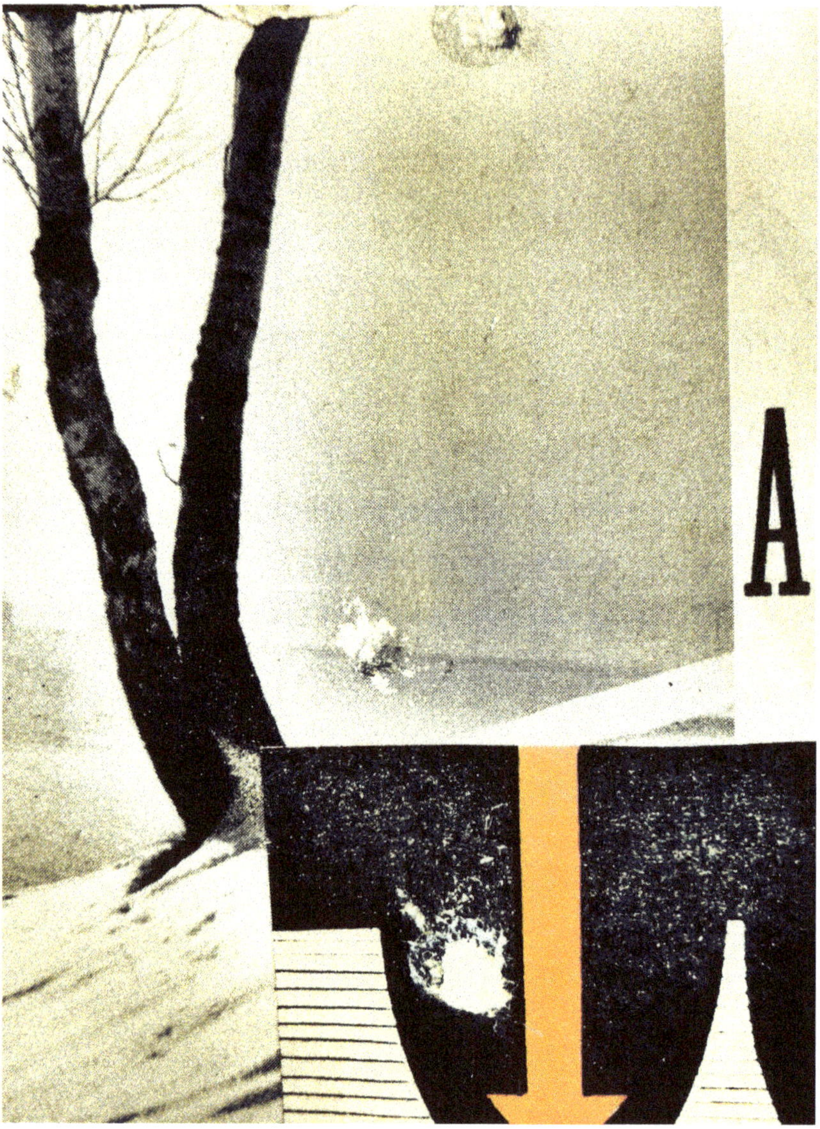
A

Trouville en automne

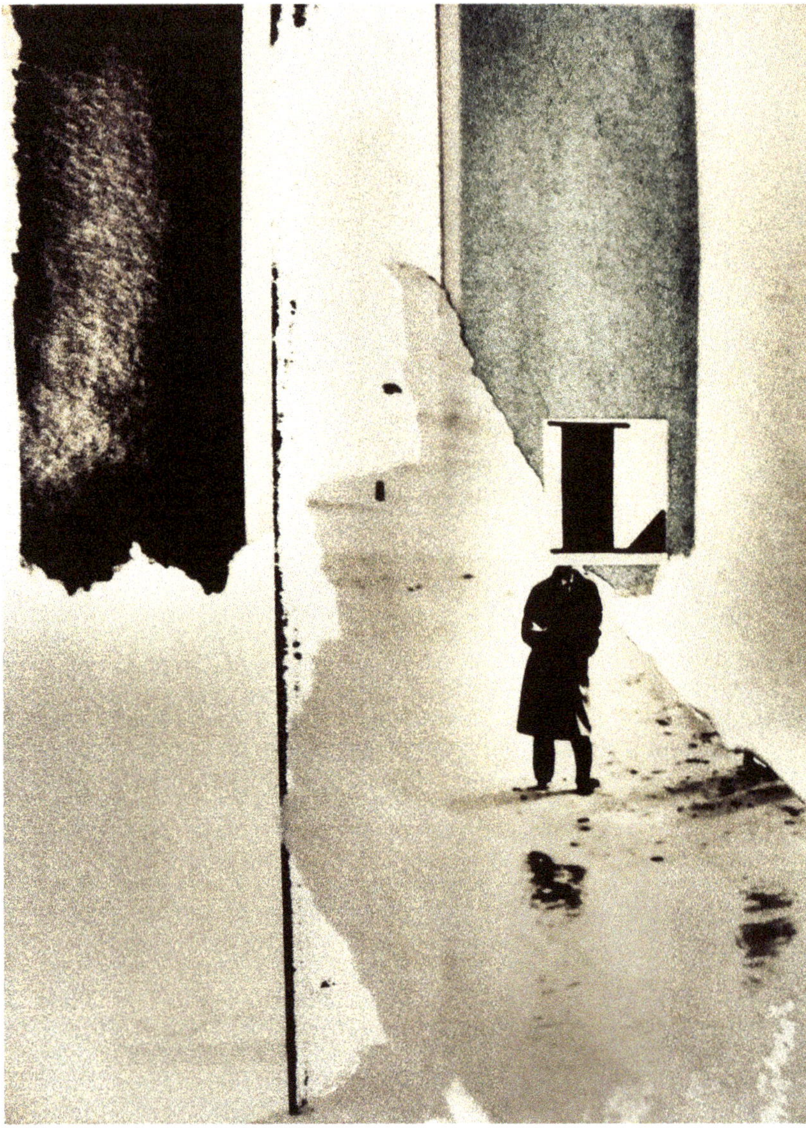
L

Waiting For The Ship "Night"

from the fogged window

MIST AND

about logbook

The works in my logbook are like automatic writings,
based on my daily life.
*
There will be specific themes and memories that
 can be used for the future.
*
By filling these pages, I'm engaging with and
acknowledging my memories.

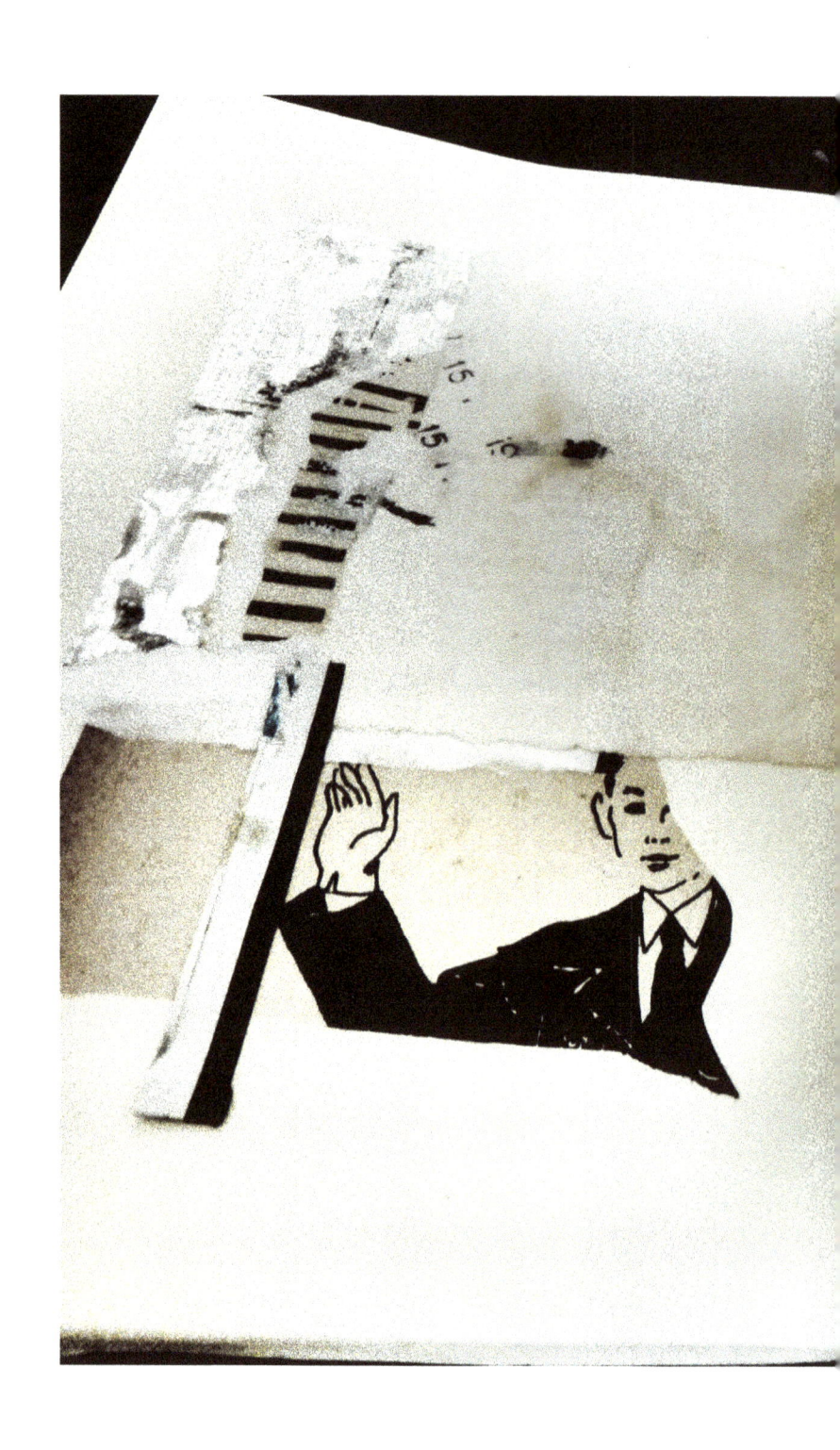

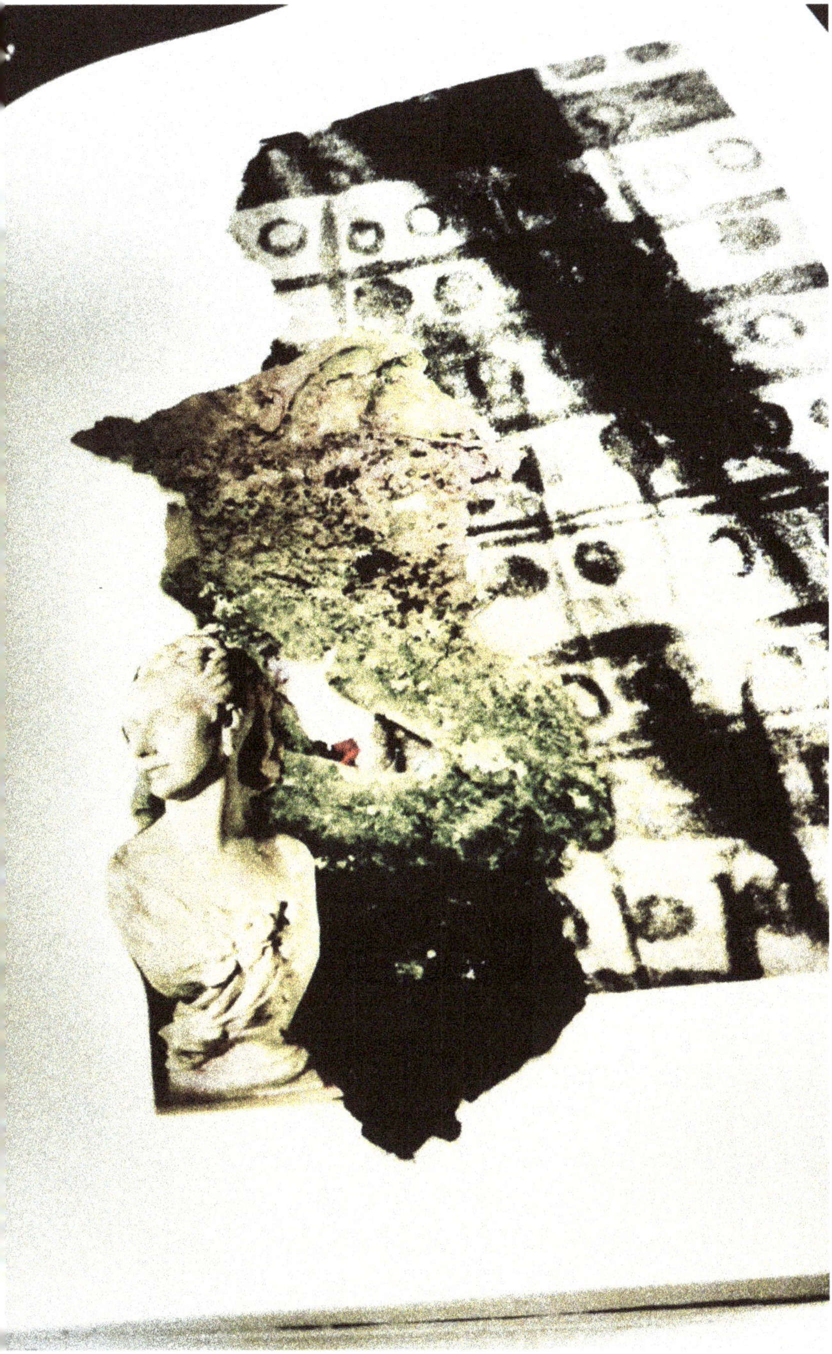

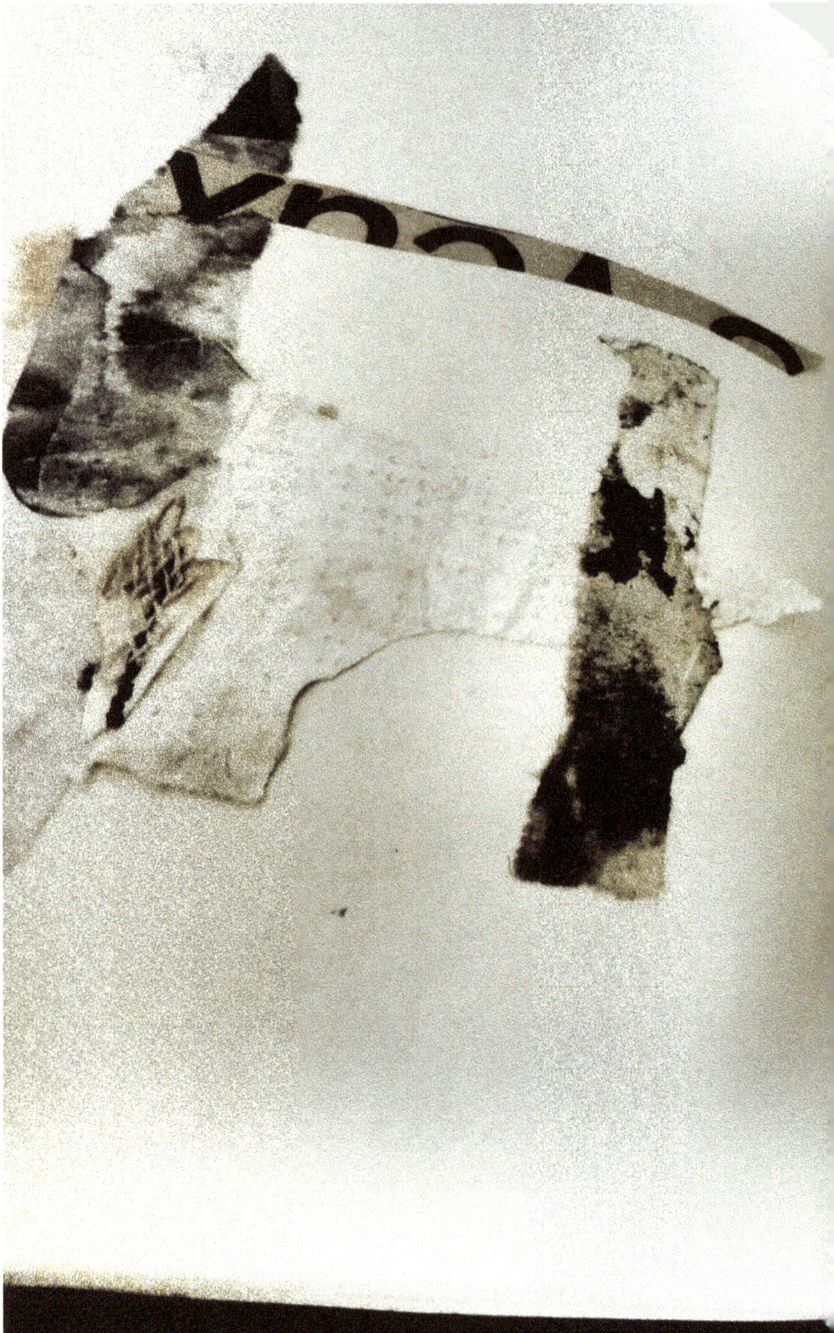

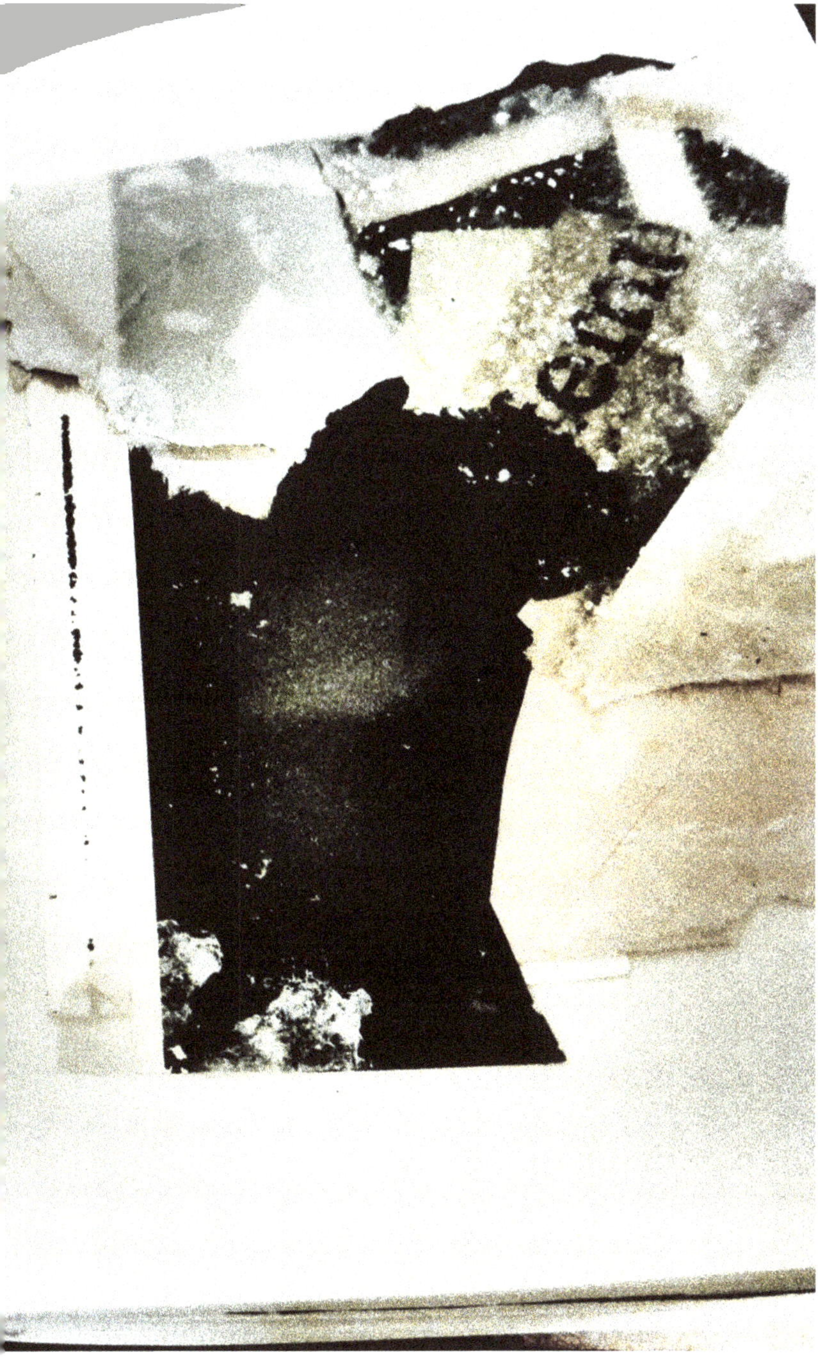

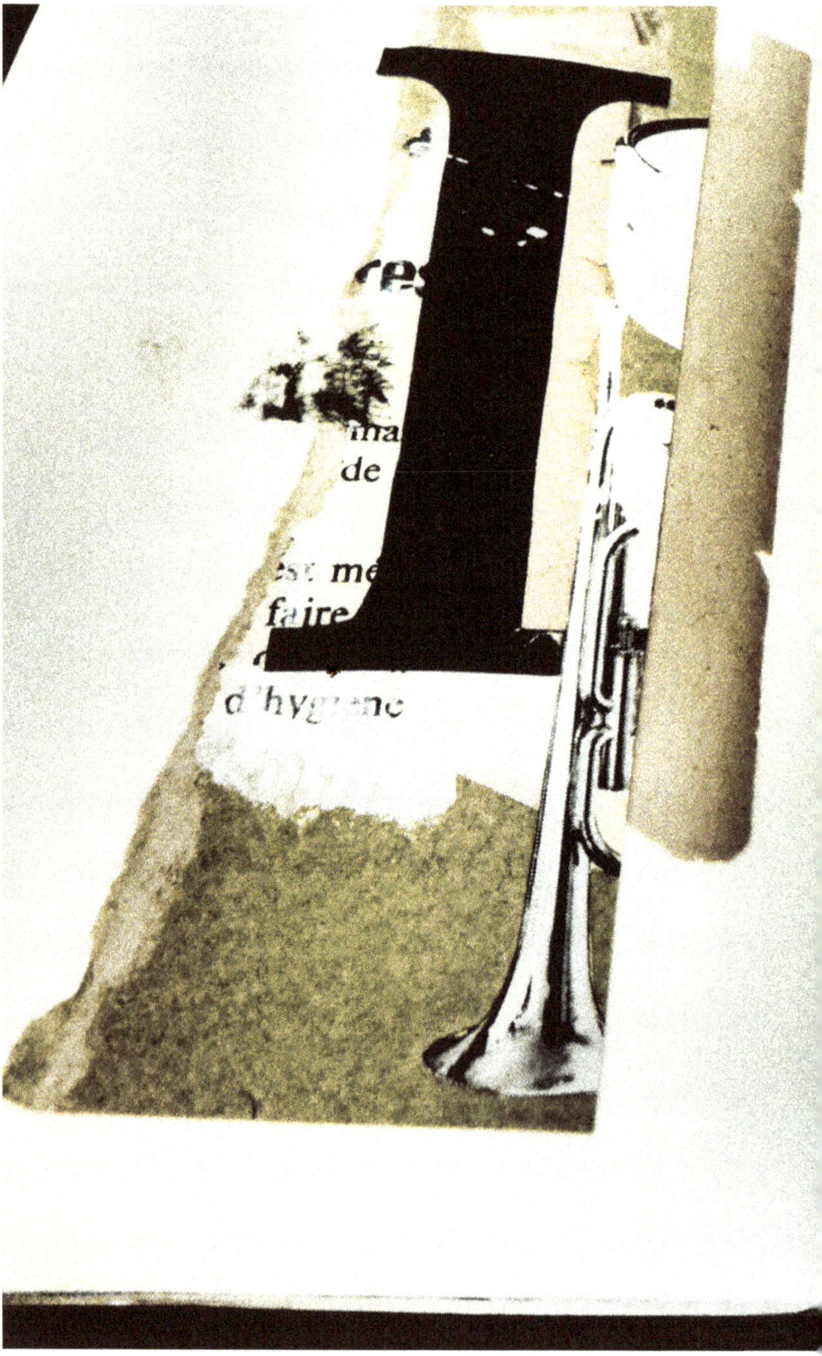
res
de
faire

Tandis que Mickey et
jouent au base-ball, un s
proche d'eux et, en voul
seigner les règles du je
balle dans la vitrine d
Les vitres volent en écl

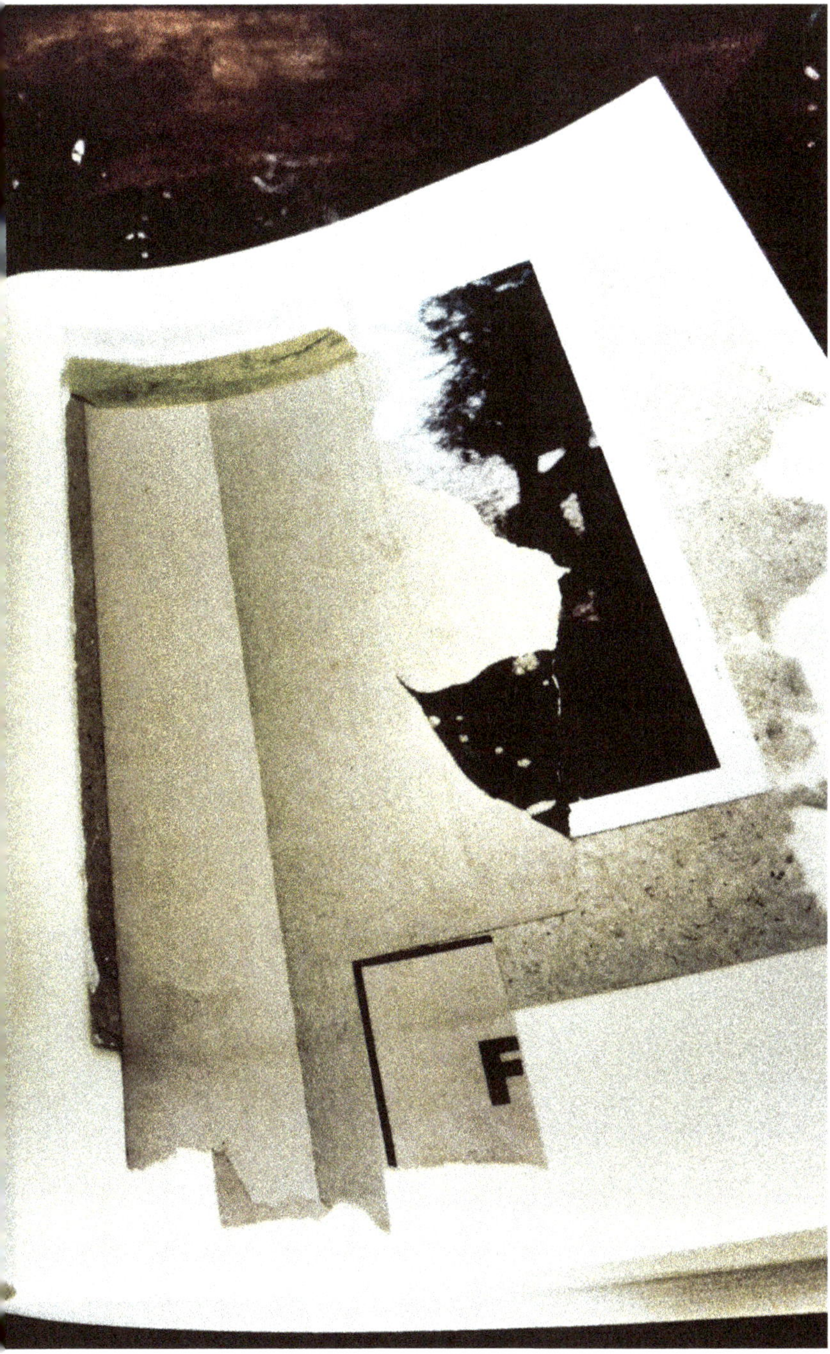
F

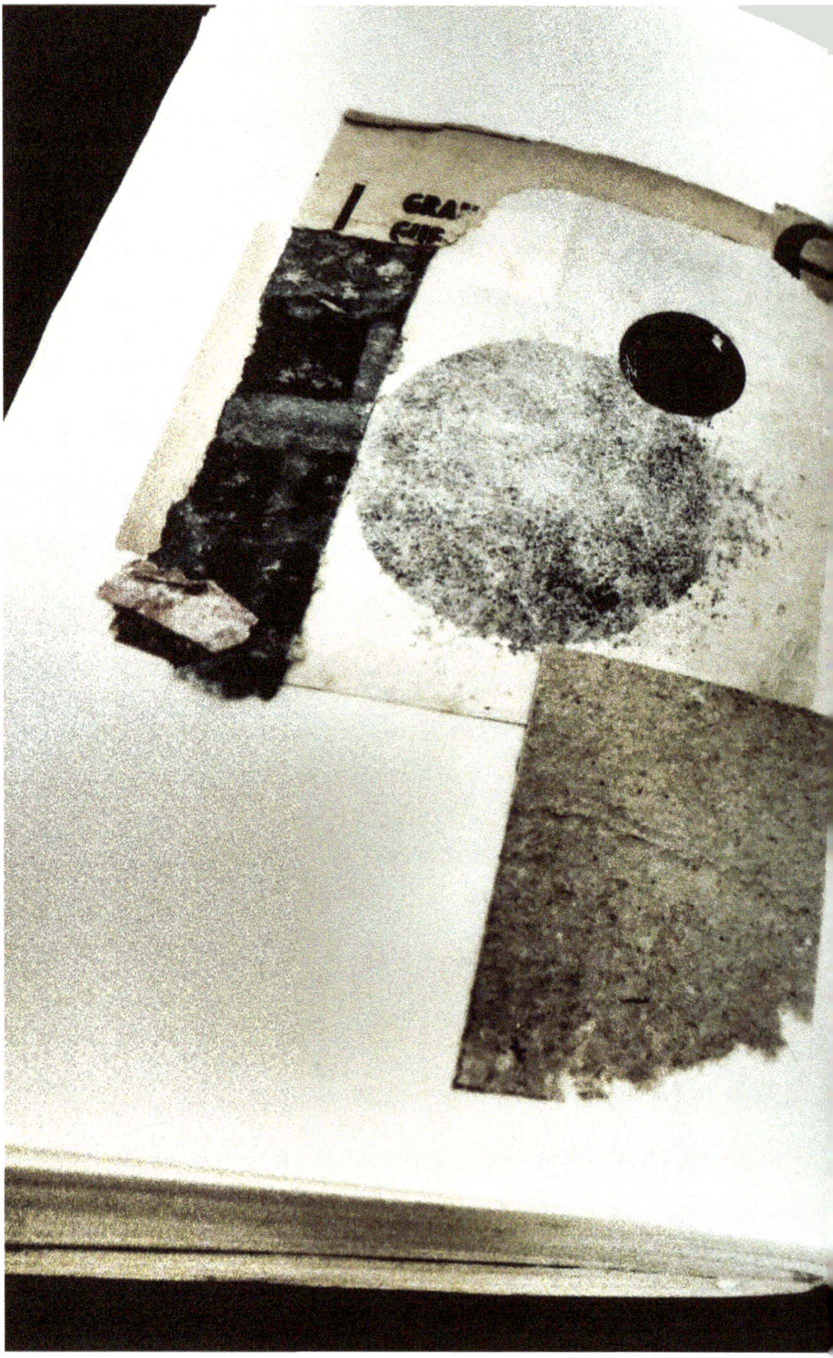

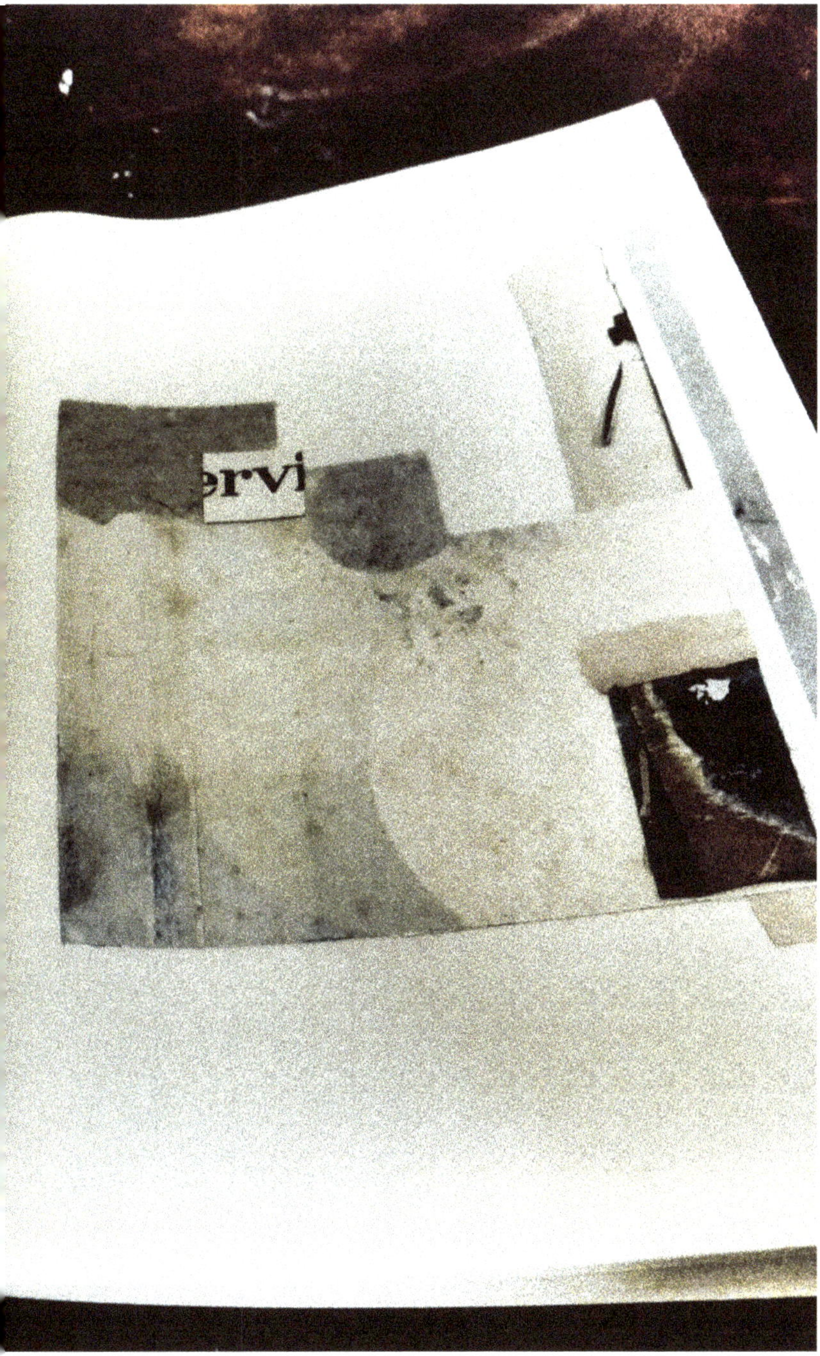
ervi

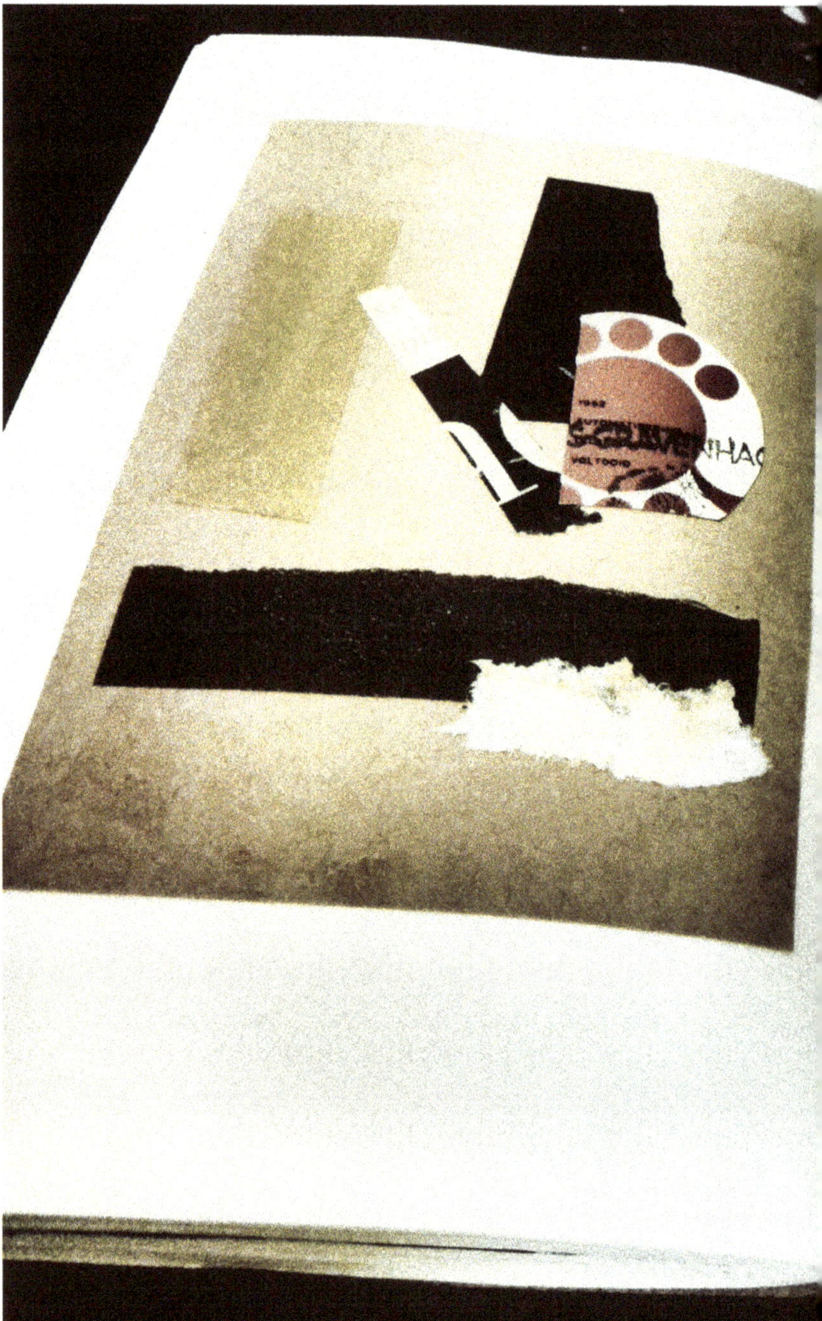

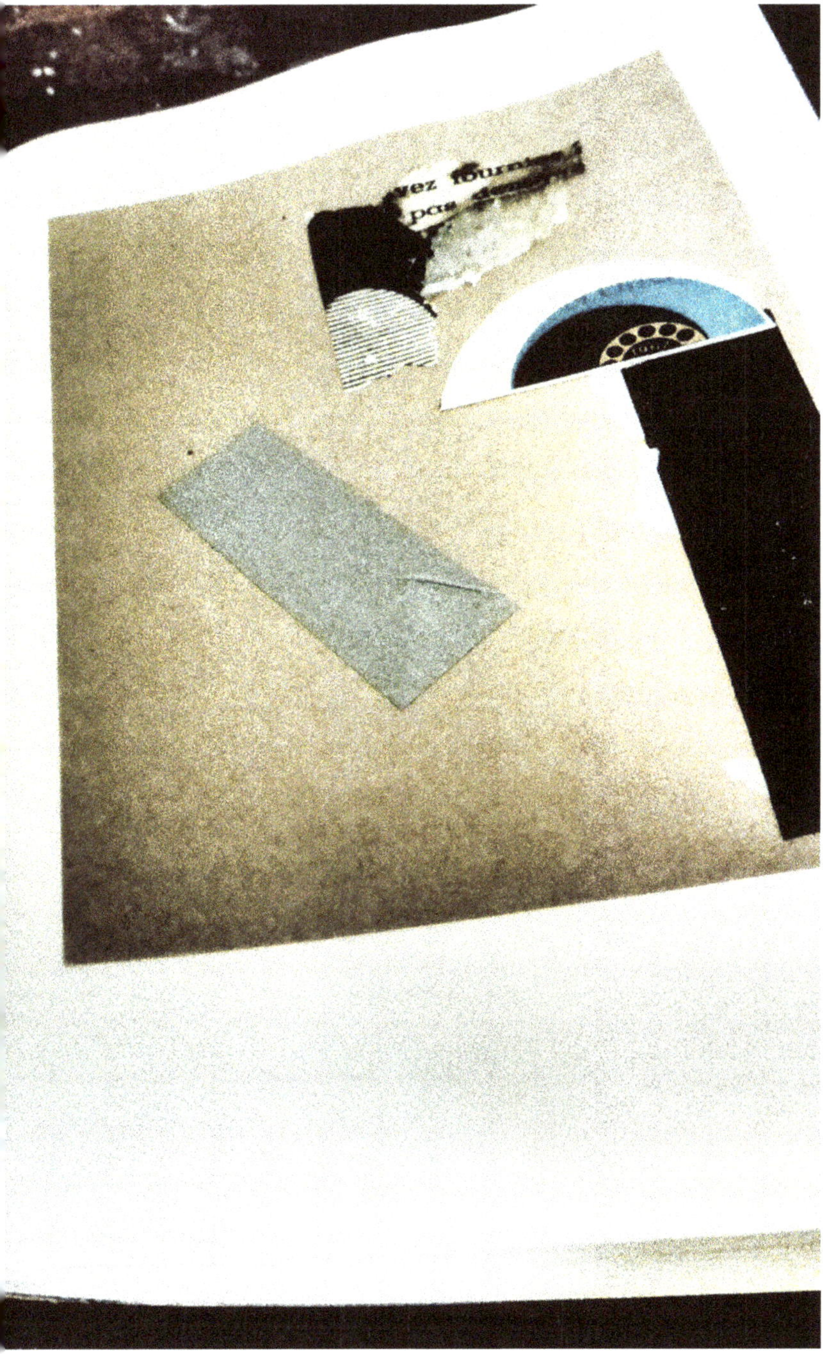

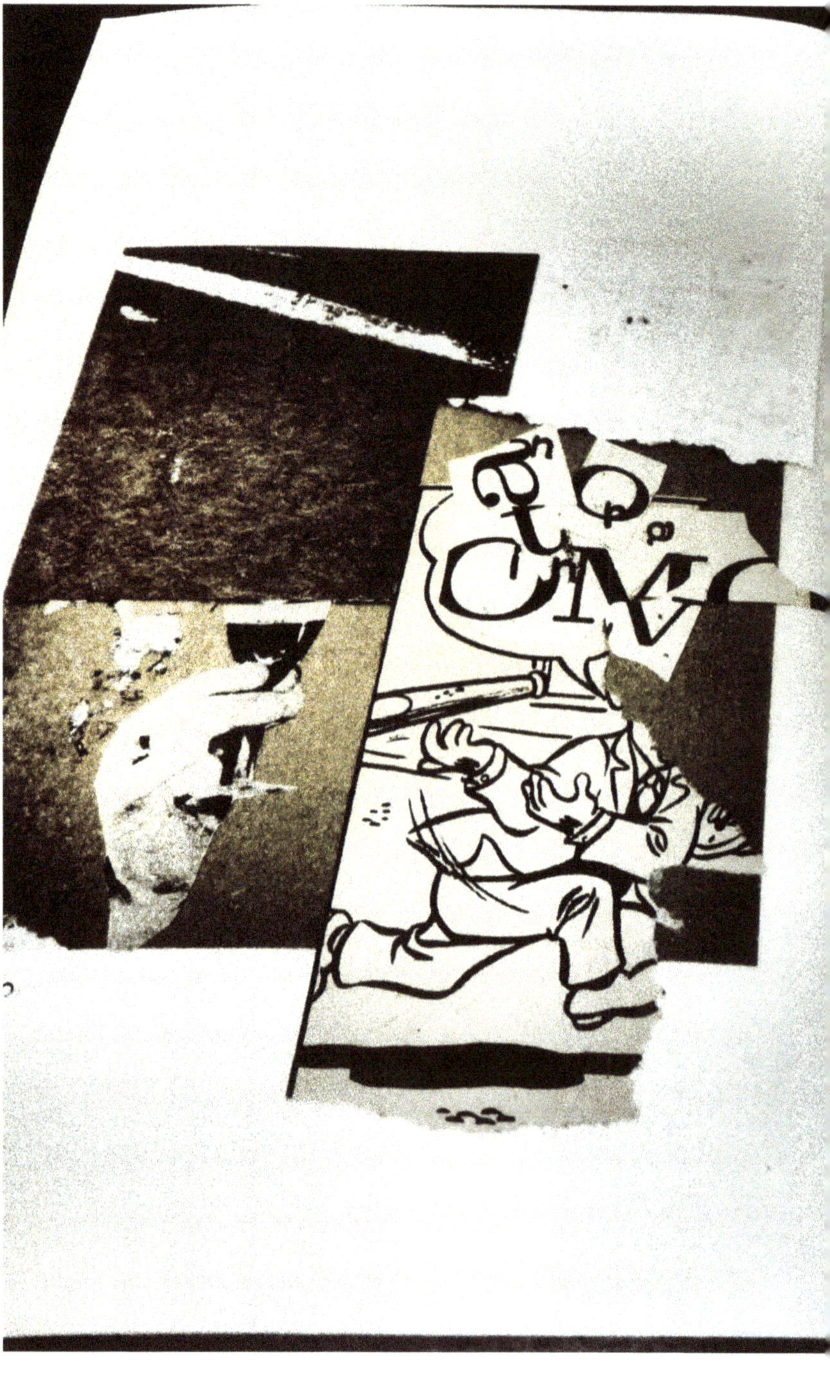

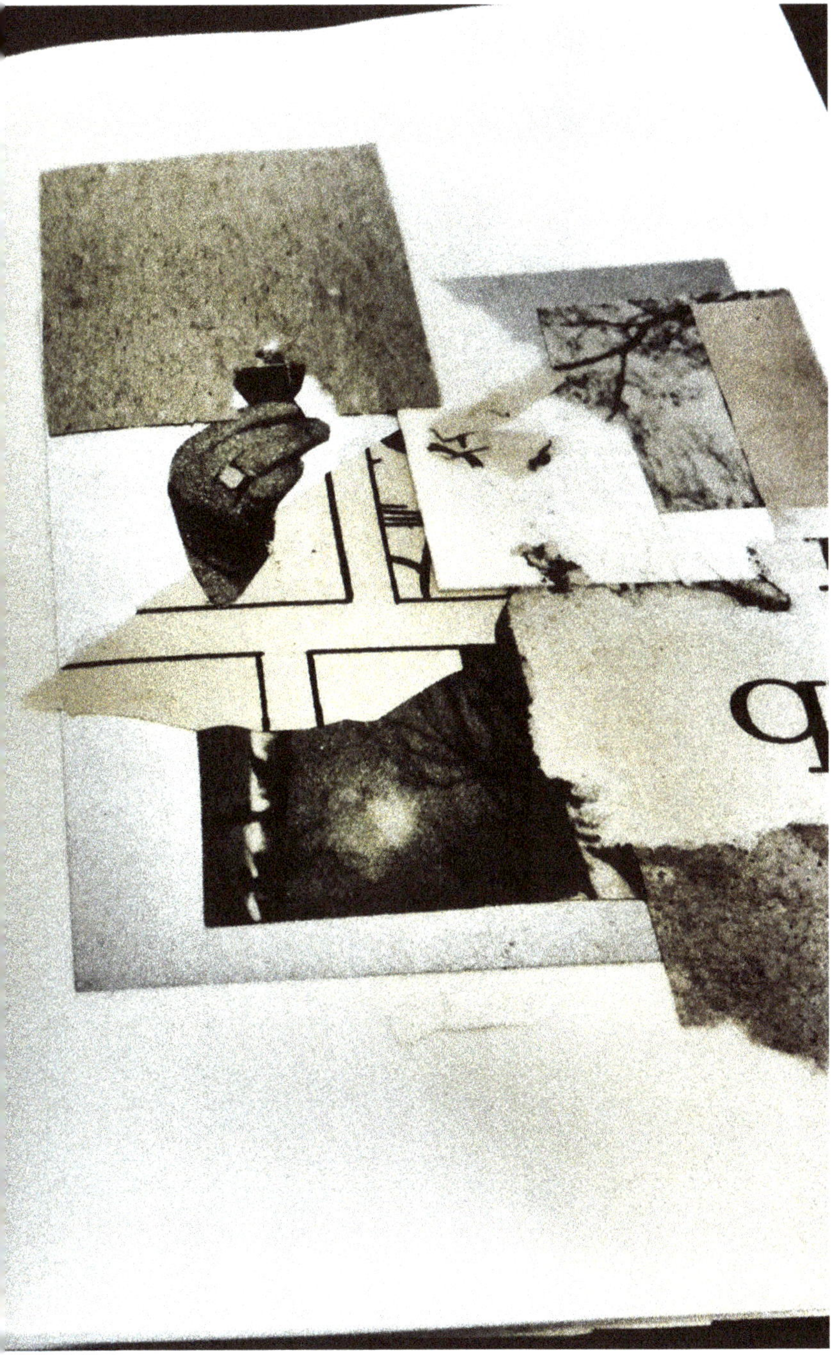

Mare Vaporum

I create collages every night before I fall asleep.
On a small notebook, pages are almost full of collages. Creation makes me forget my sorrow and despair. When the work is finished I look up at the moon from my window. The moon also looks at the people floating on the pillow as vapor of the sea. I hope everyone will enjoy my pieces and have nice dreams.

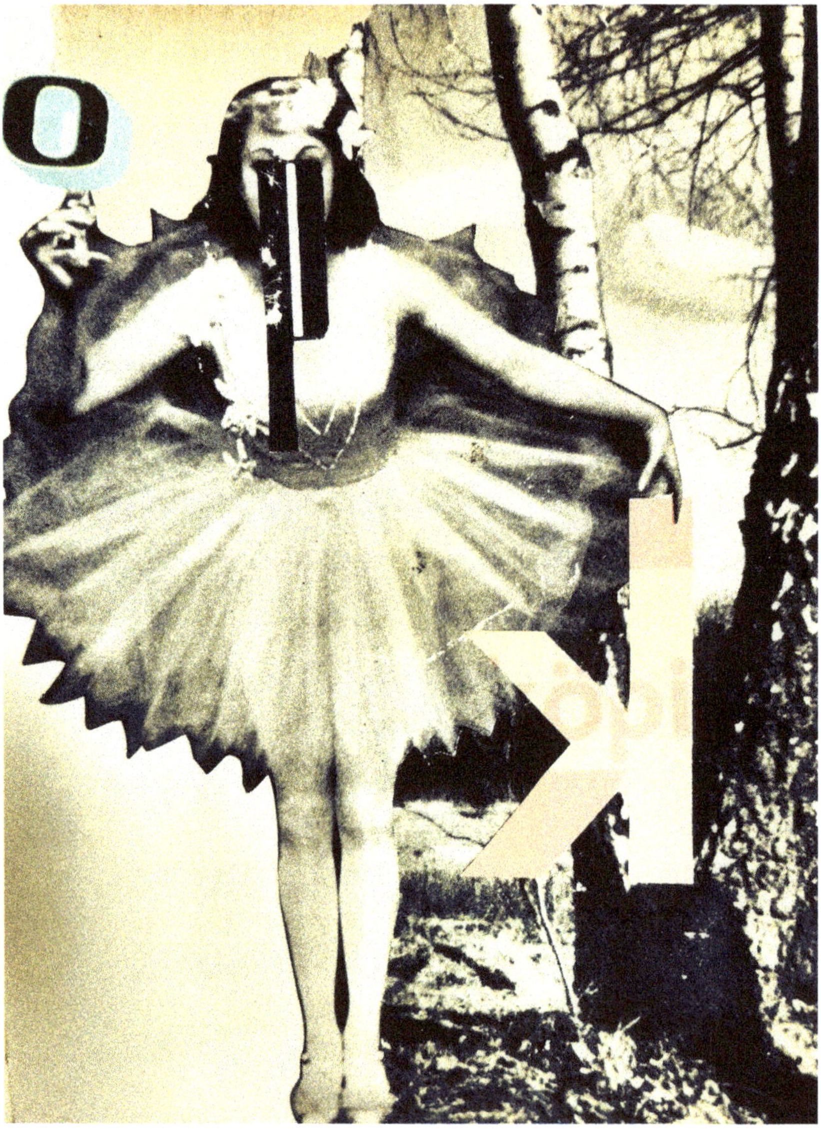
O

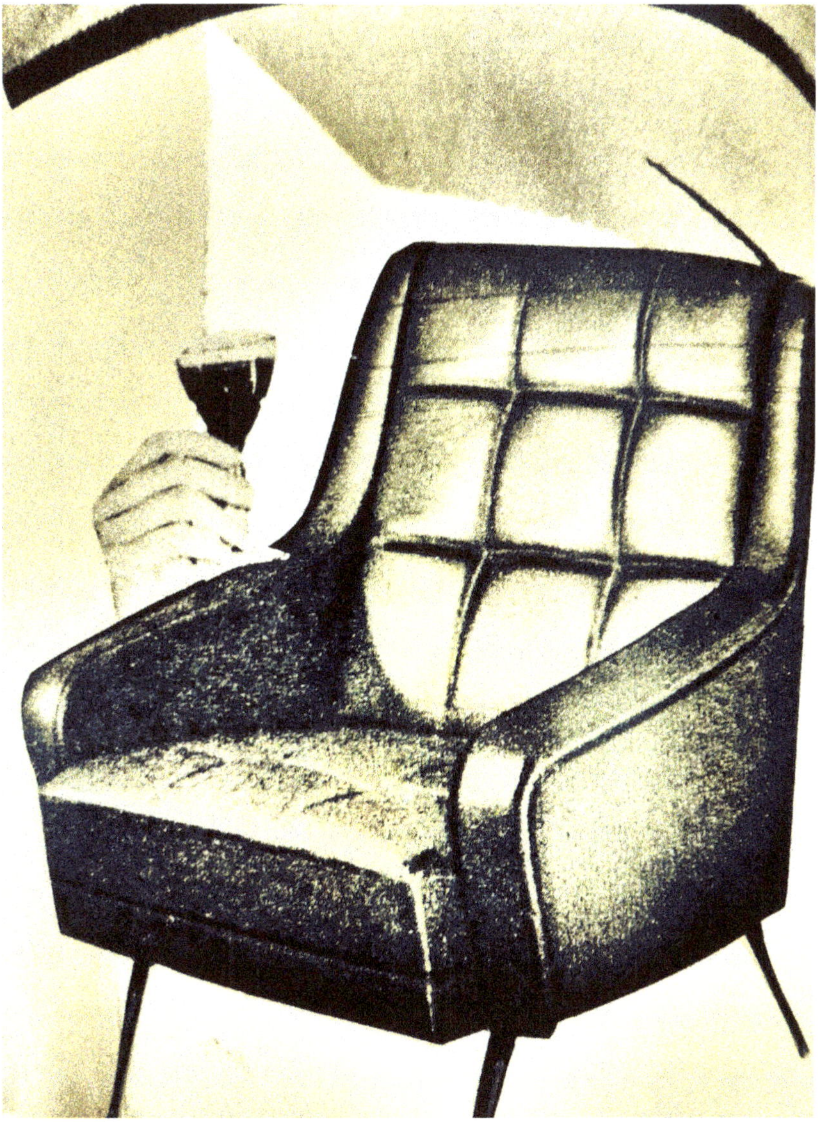

elle
vec mesure.
resta interloqué. Elle
Artuprésent. flûtes Perrier Jouet, tasse Rita Kim.

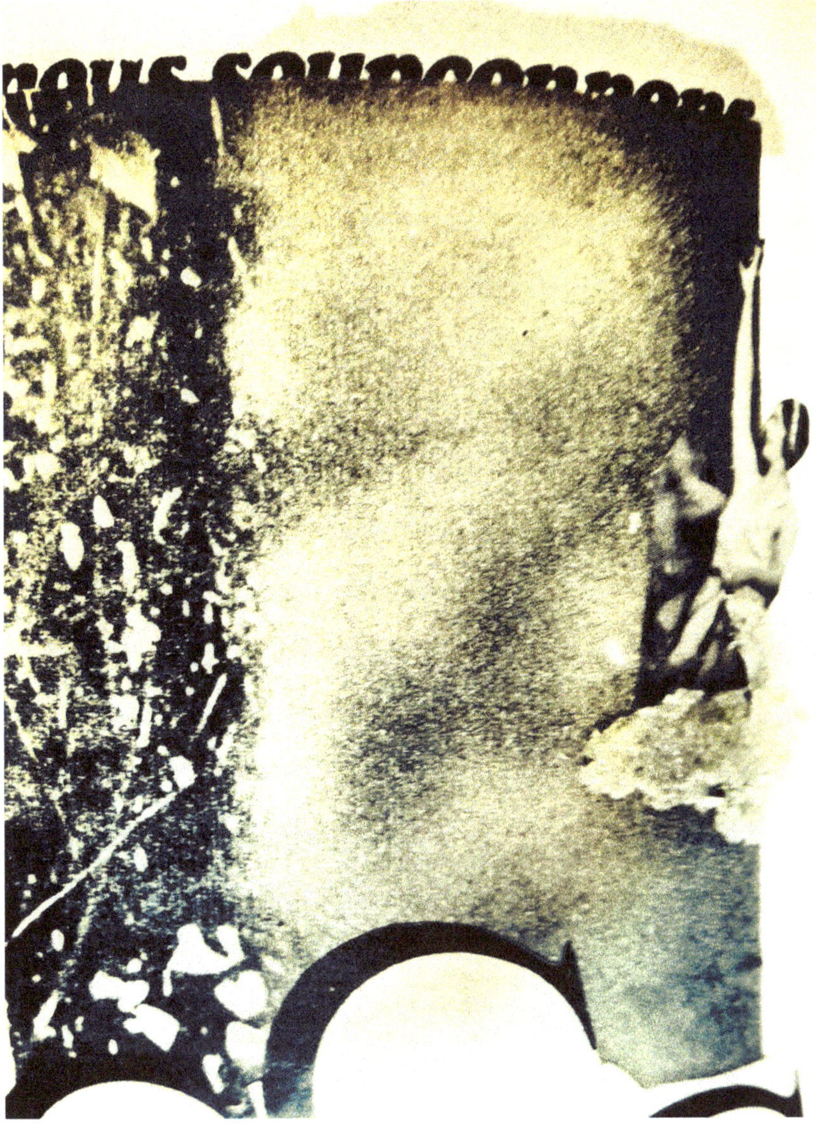

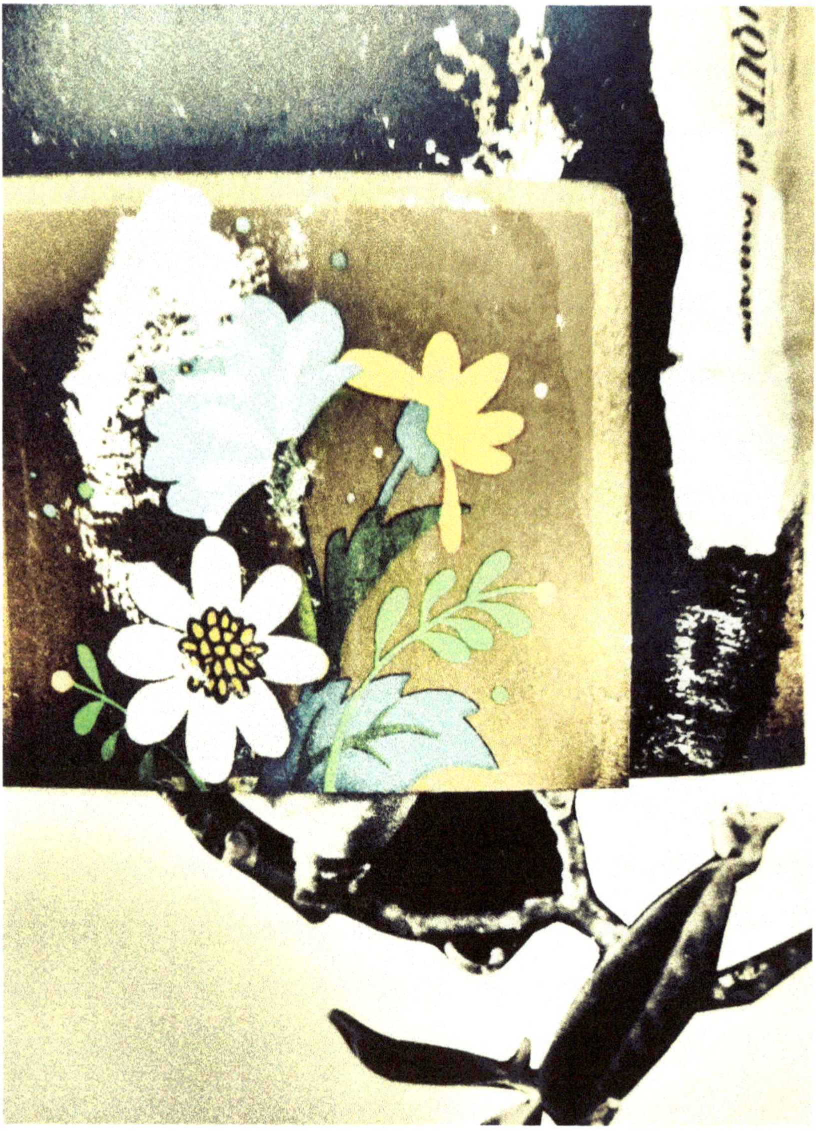

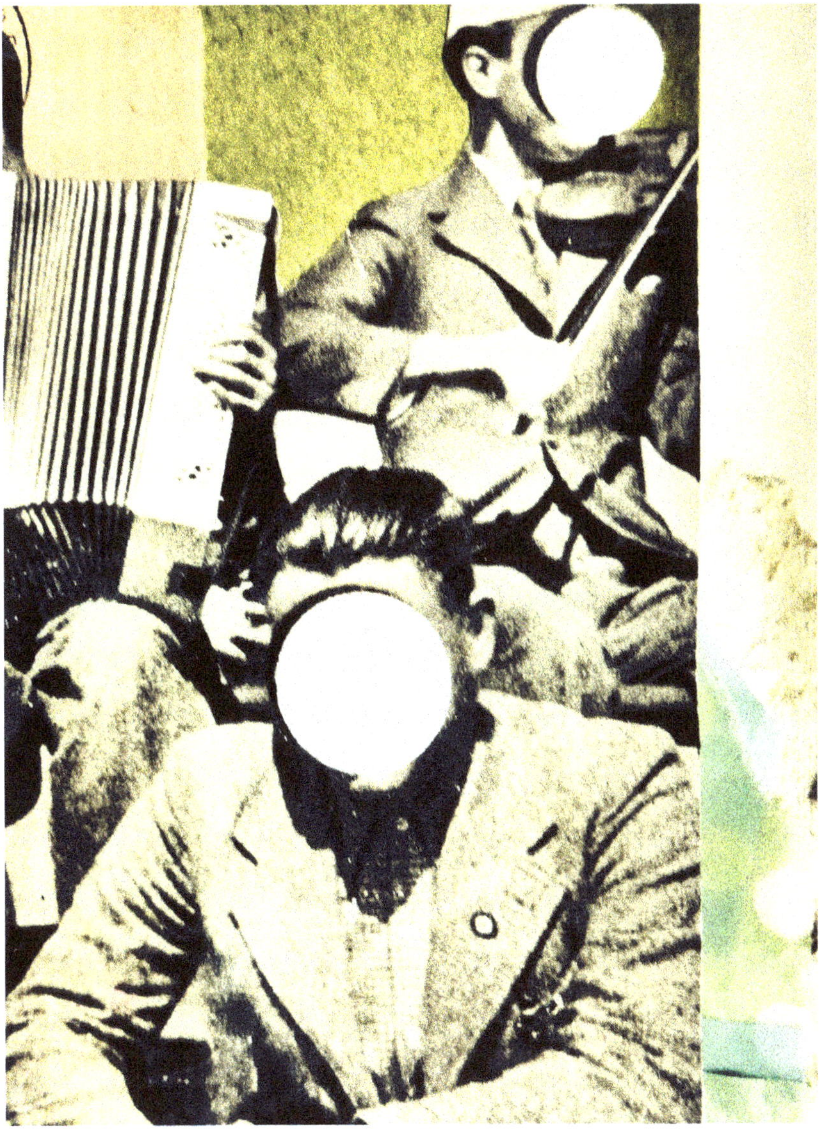

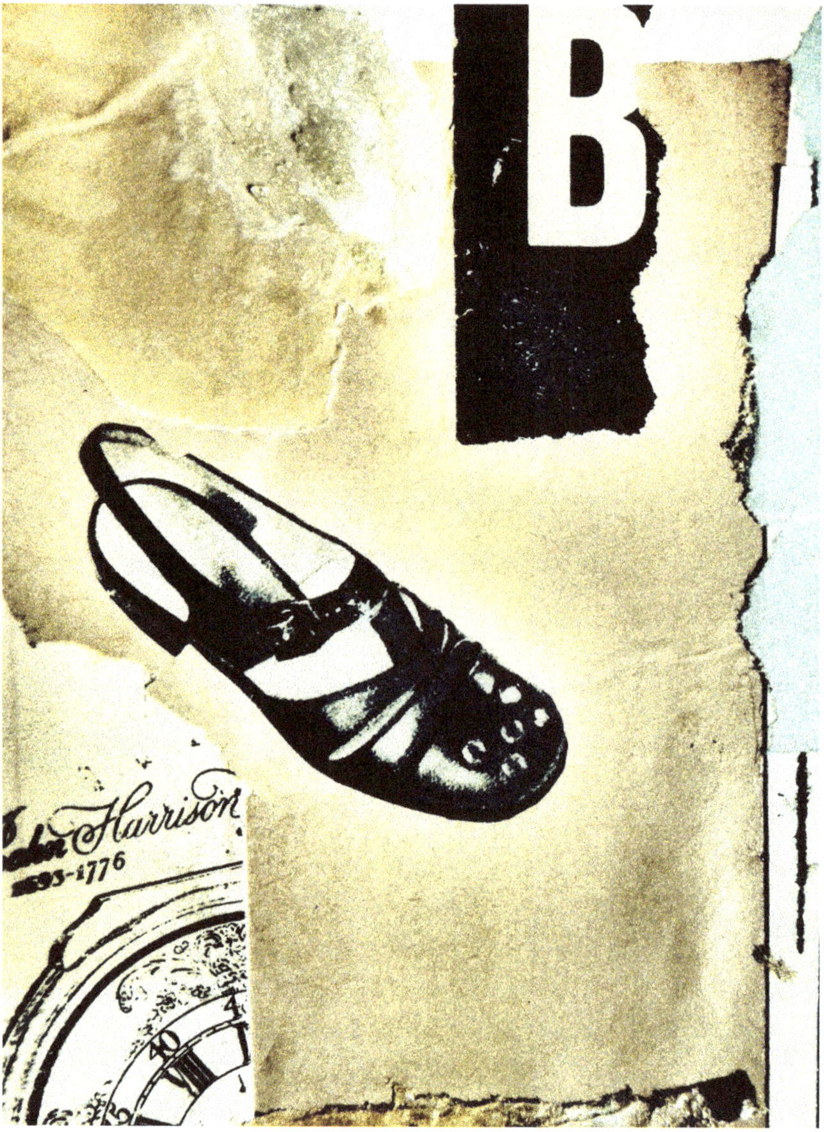
B
Harrison
1693-1776

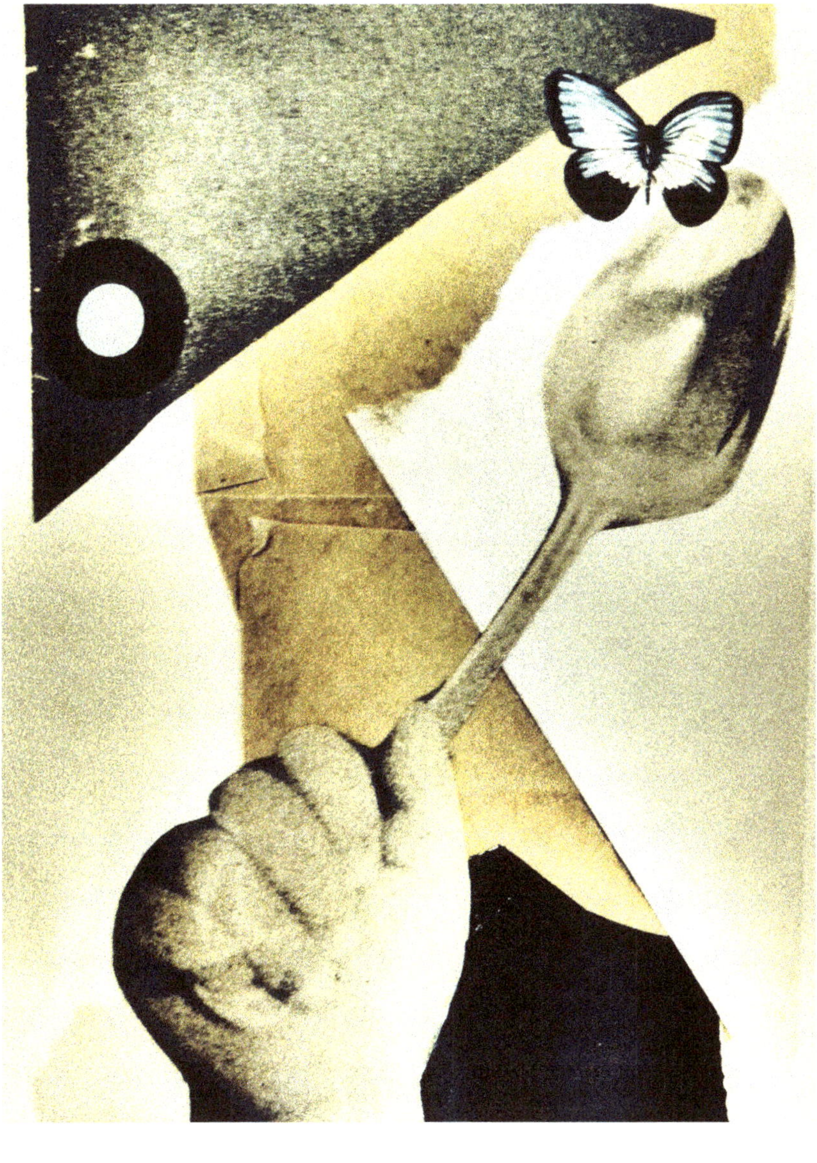

au dos.
d'emmanchures sur l'envers et les f
parementures. Assembler dos et 1/2 devants
froncer la taille. Réunir corsage e jupe.
les parementures.
s. Piqûrer sur 5 rang serrés

Post It

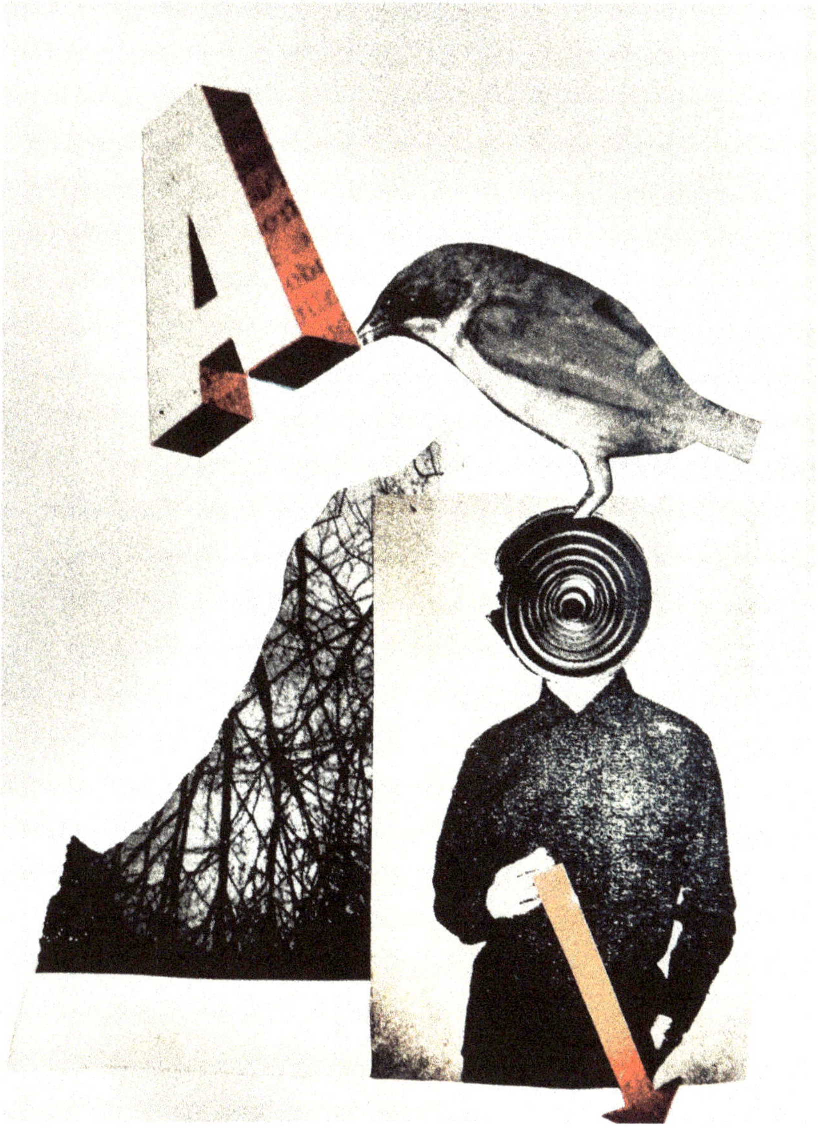

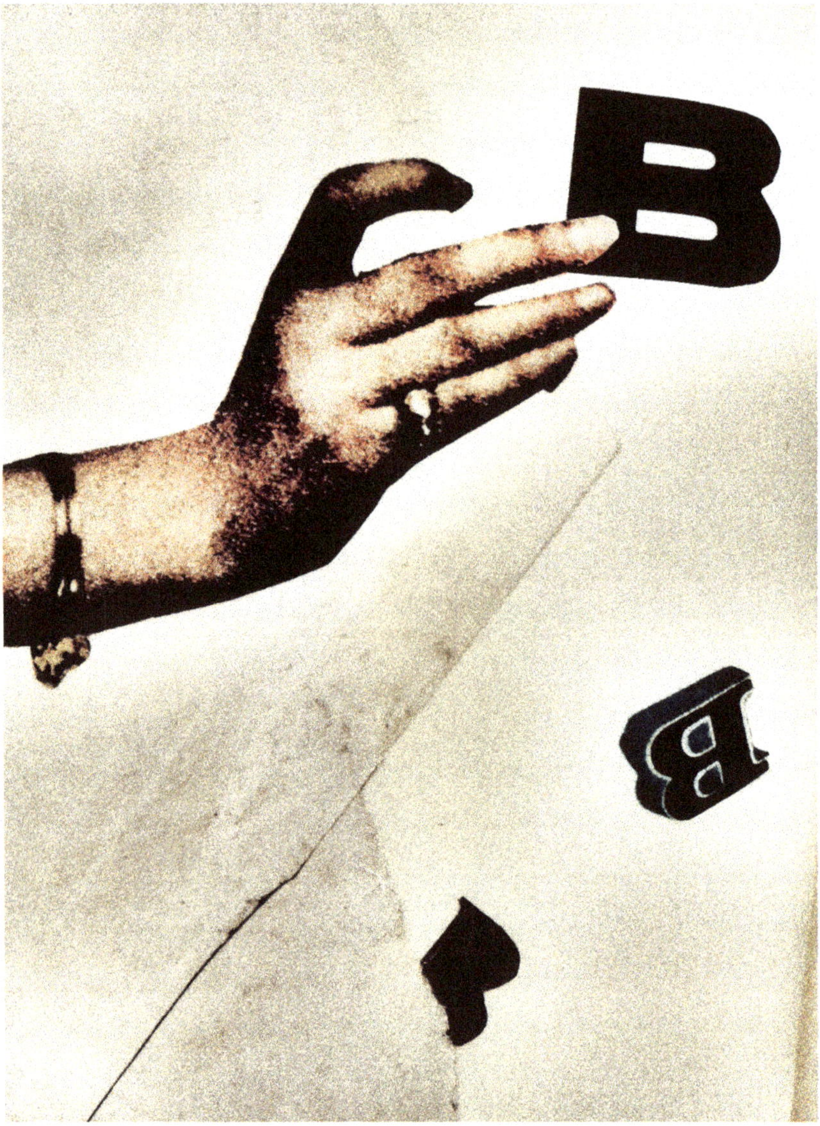
B
B

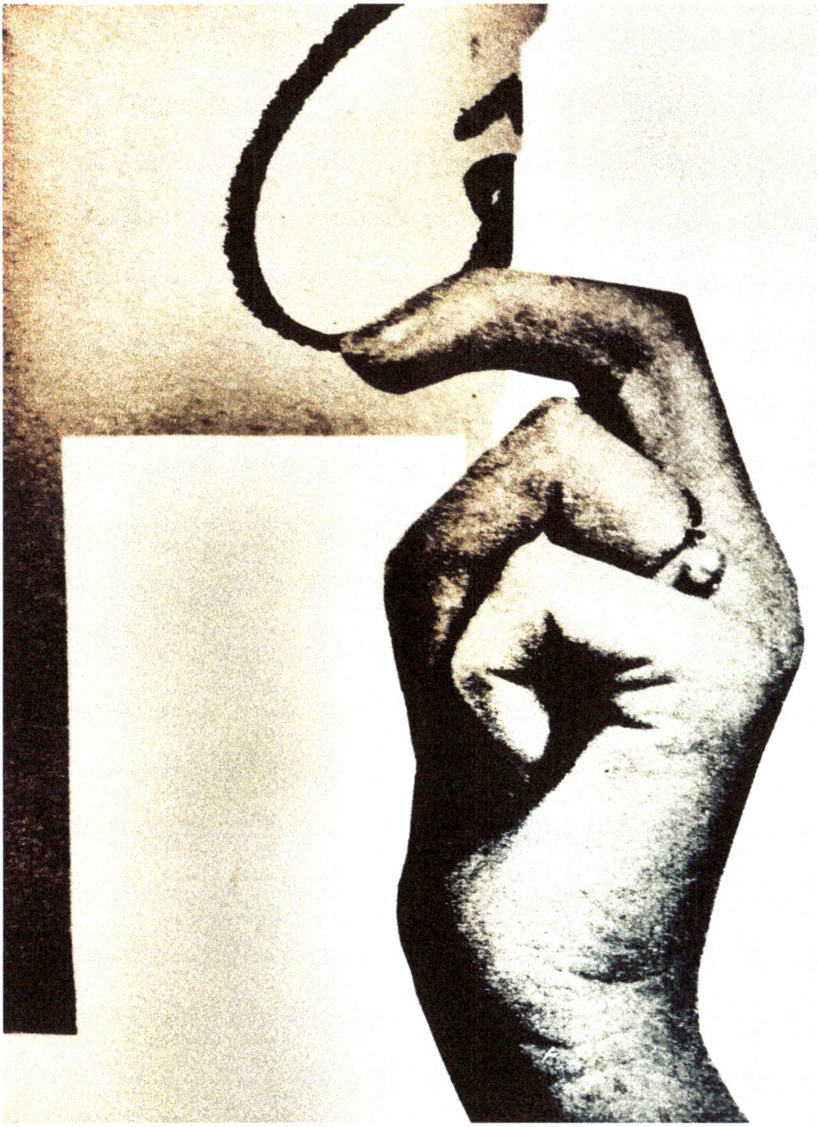

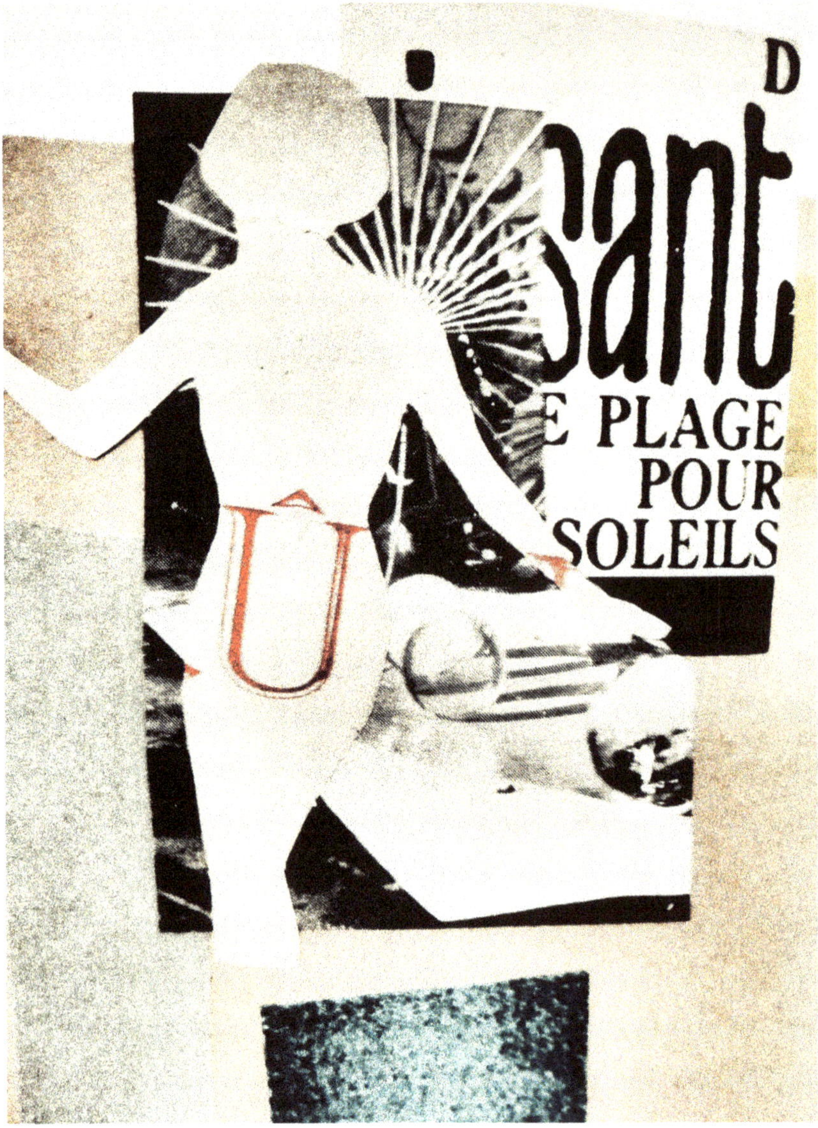
D
sant
E PLAGE
POUR
SOLEILS

ON TH

The seasons

The seasons are similar to a Merry-Go-Round.
On the beach during the winter,
a chill breeze reminds the wagon a cry.
It's an ecstatic scream of delight in the summer.

58

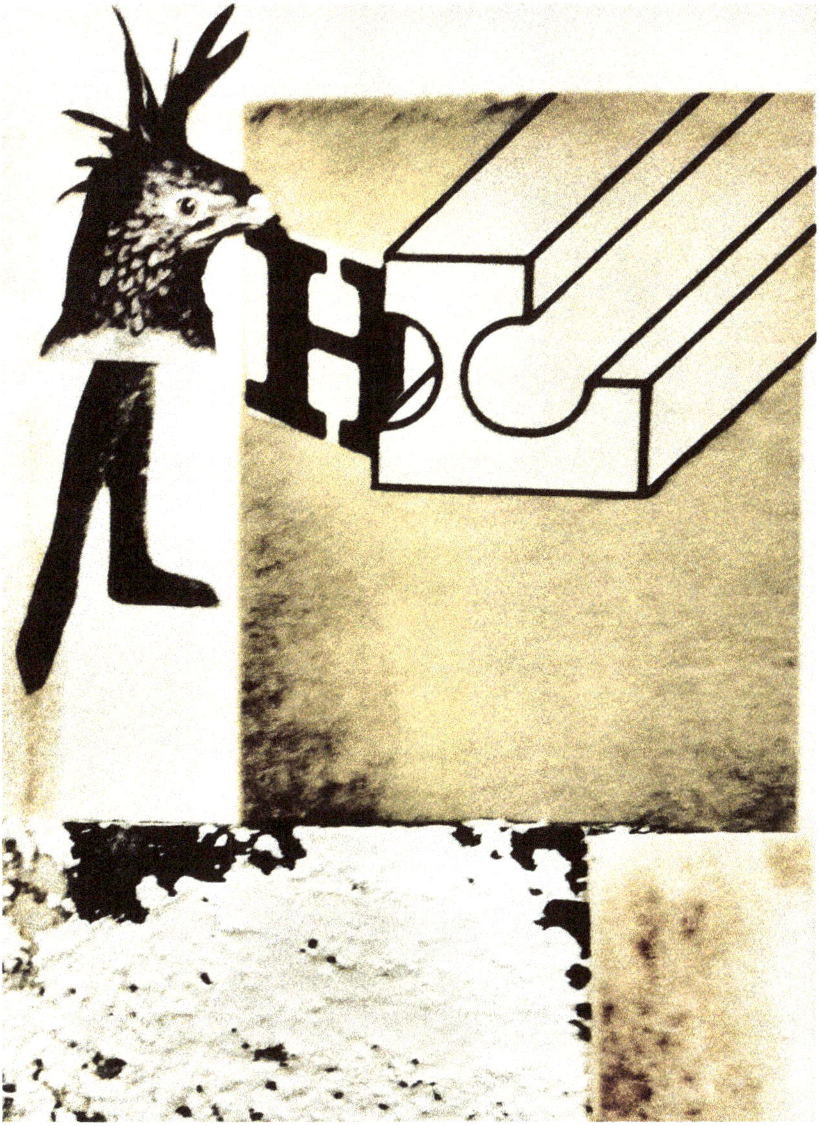

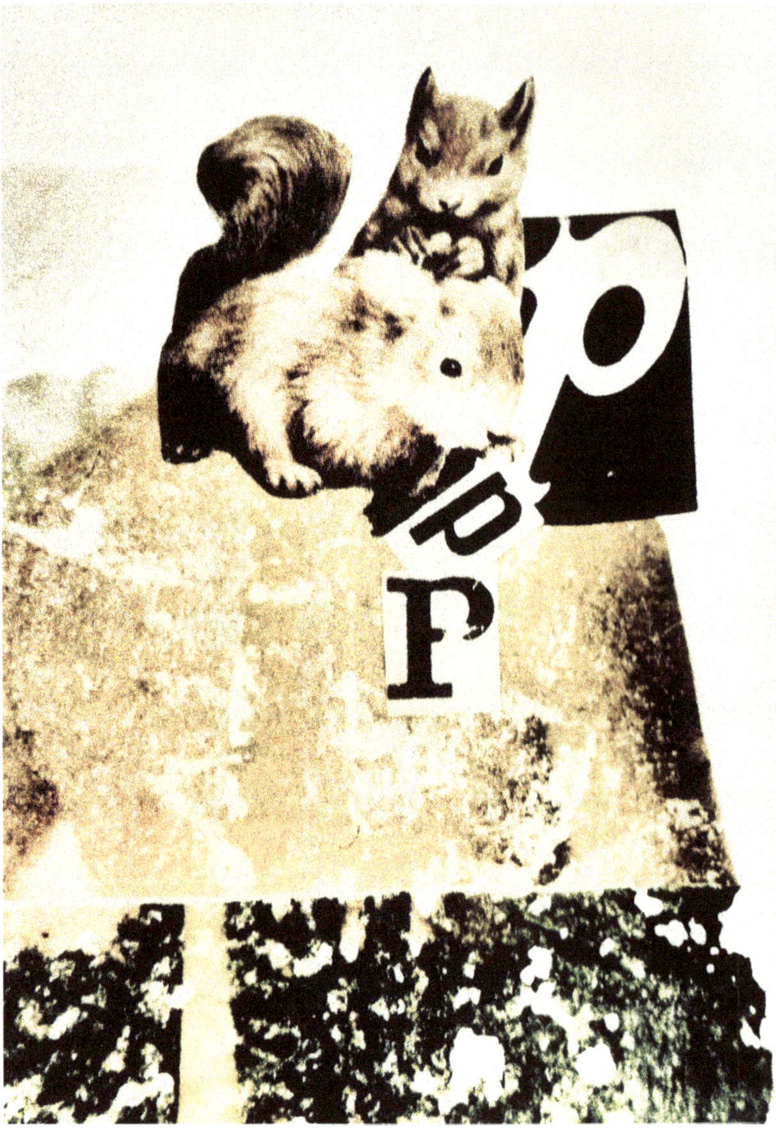

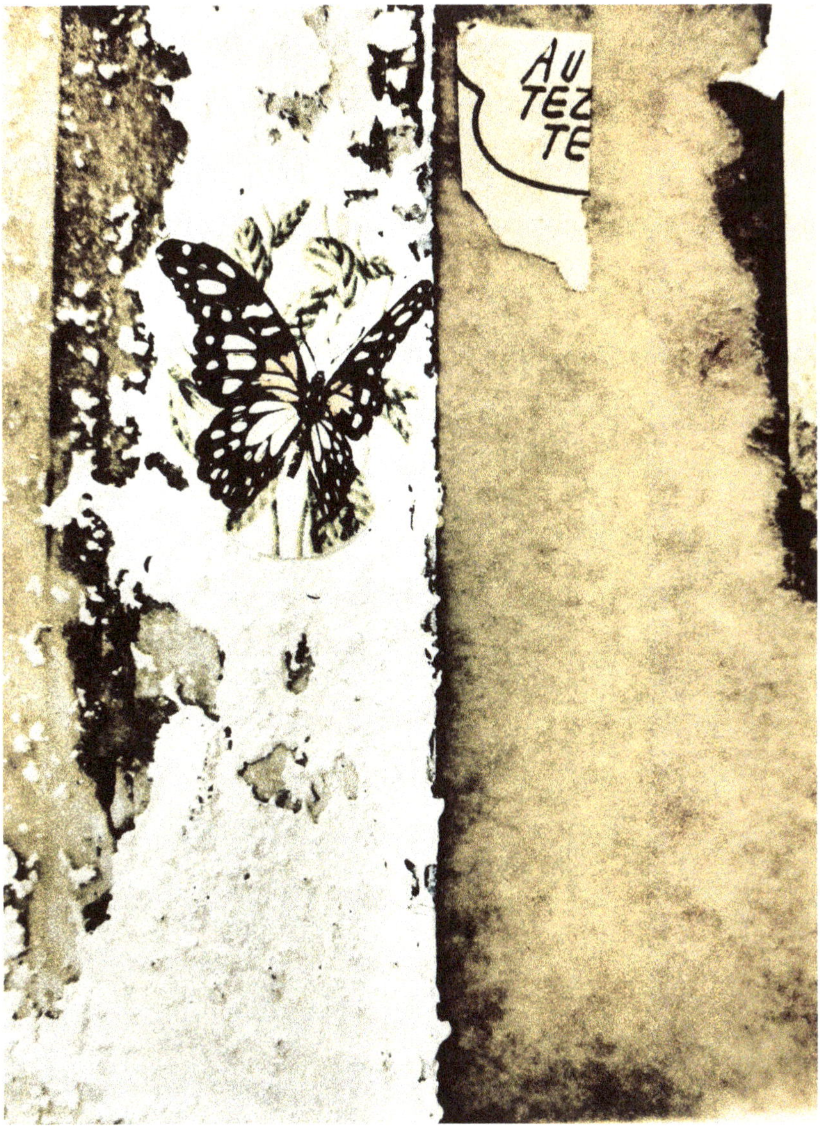
AU
TEZ
TE

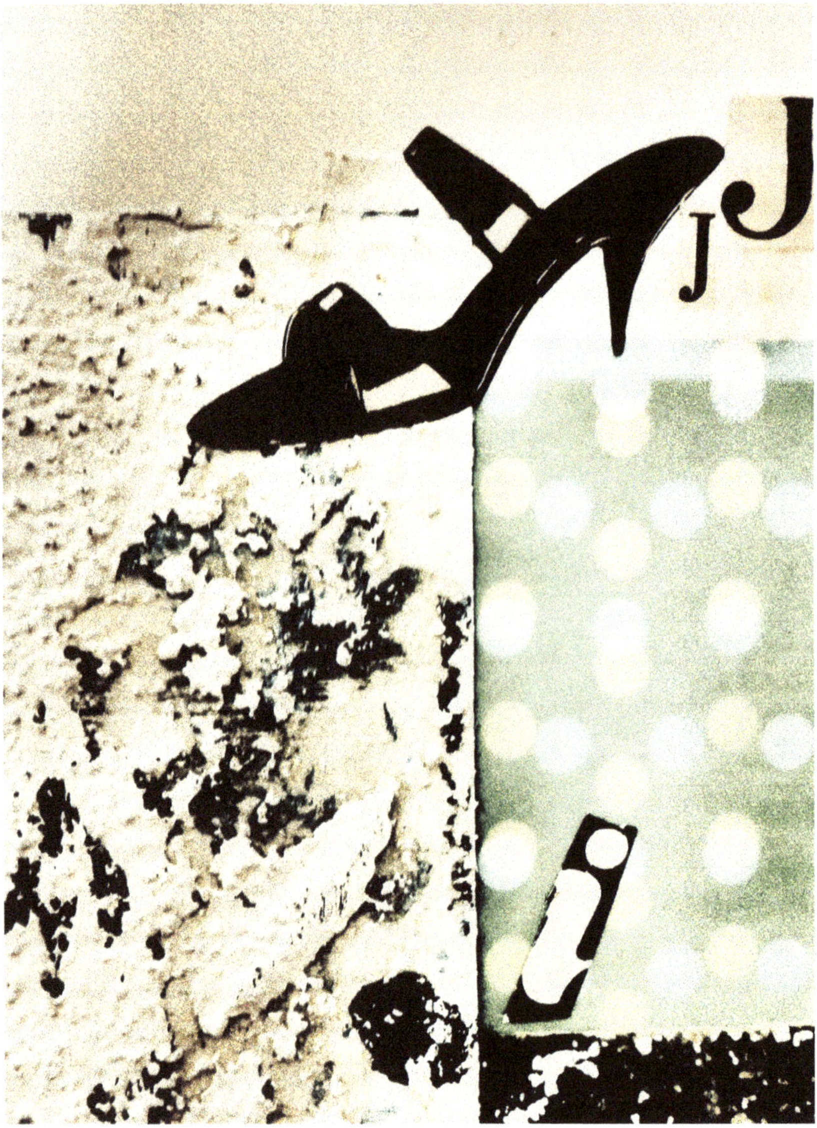
J
J
i

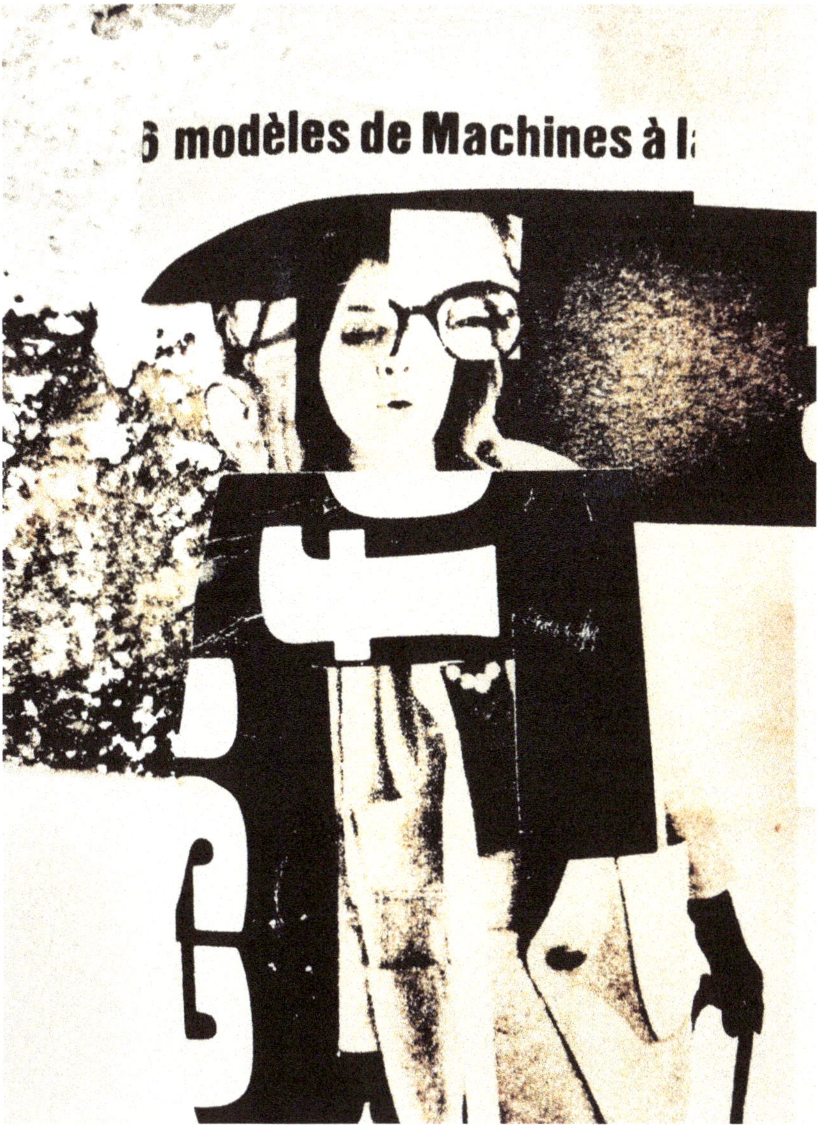
6 modèles de Machines à la

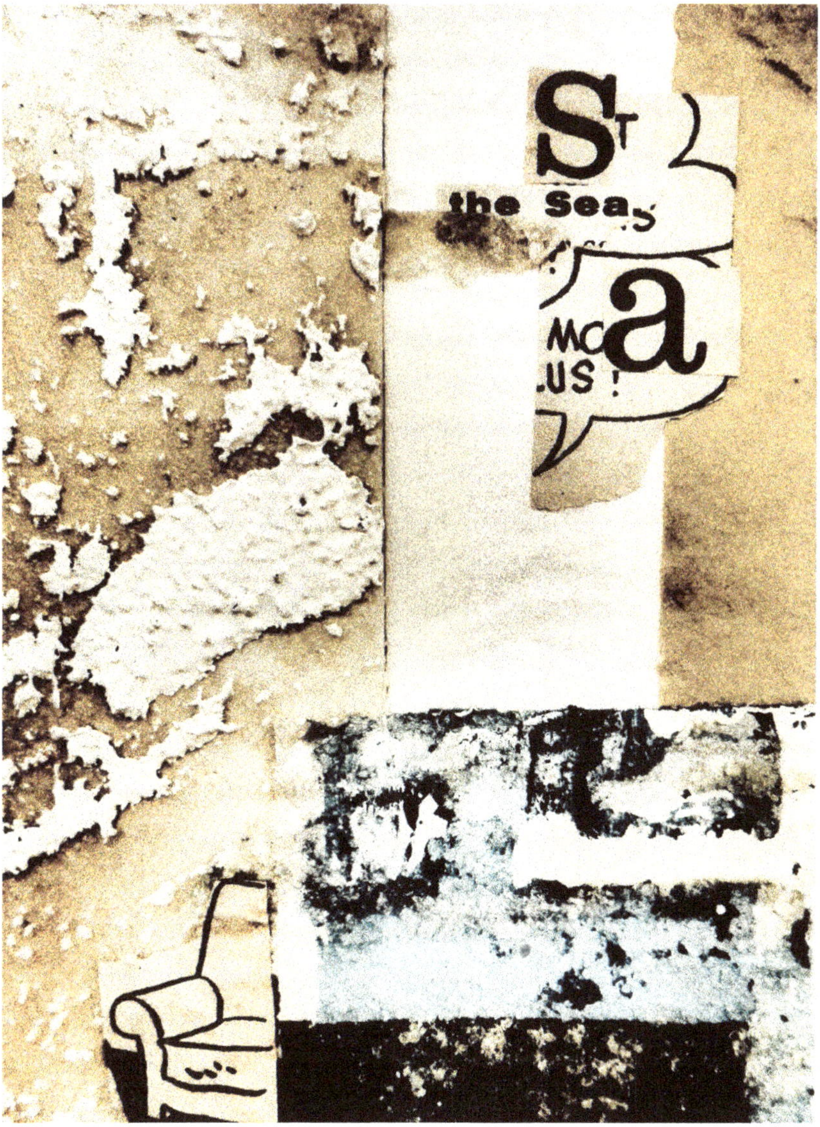

St
the Sea
MC
LUS !
a

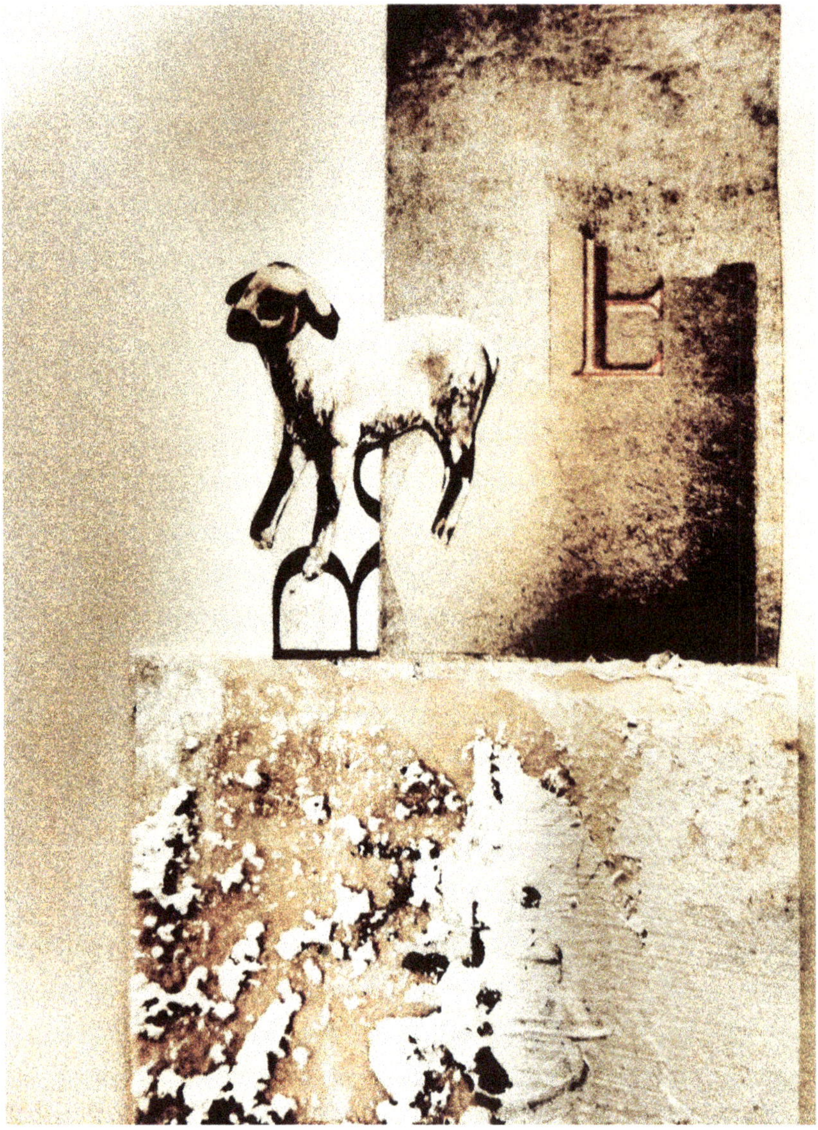

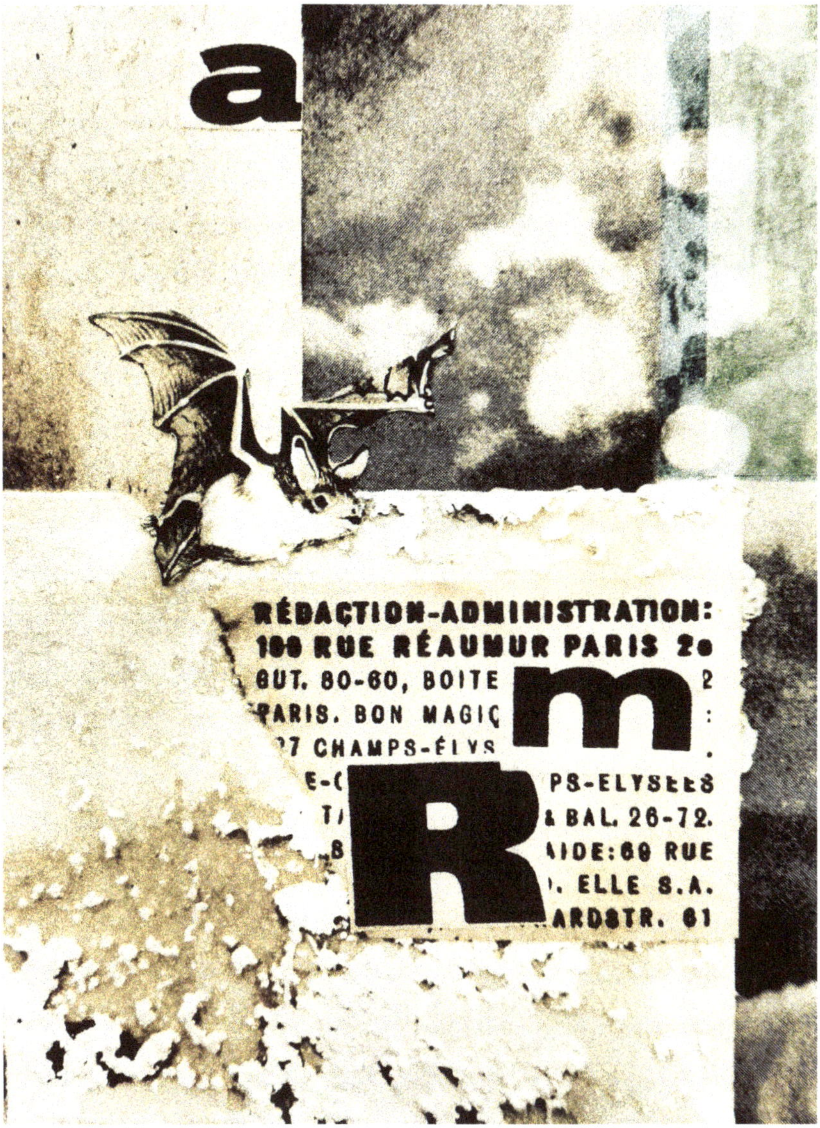
a
RÉDACTION-ADMINISTRATION:
100 RUE RÉAUMUR PARIS 2e
GUT. 80-60, BOITE
PARIS. BON MAGIÇ
27 CHAMPS-ÉLYS
PS-ELYSEES
BAL. 26-72.
AIDE: 60 RUE
ELLE S.A.
ARDSTR. 61
m
R

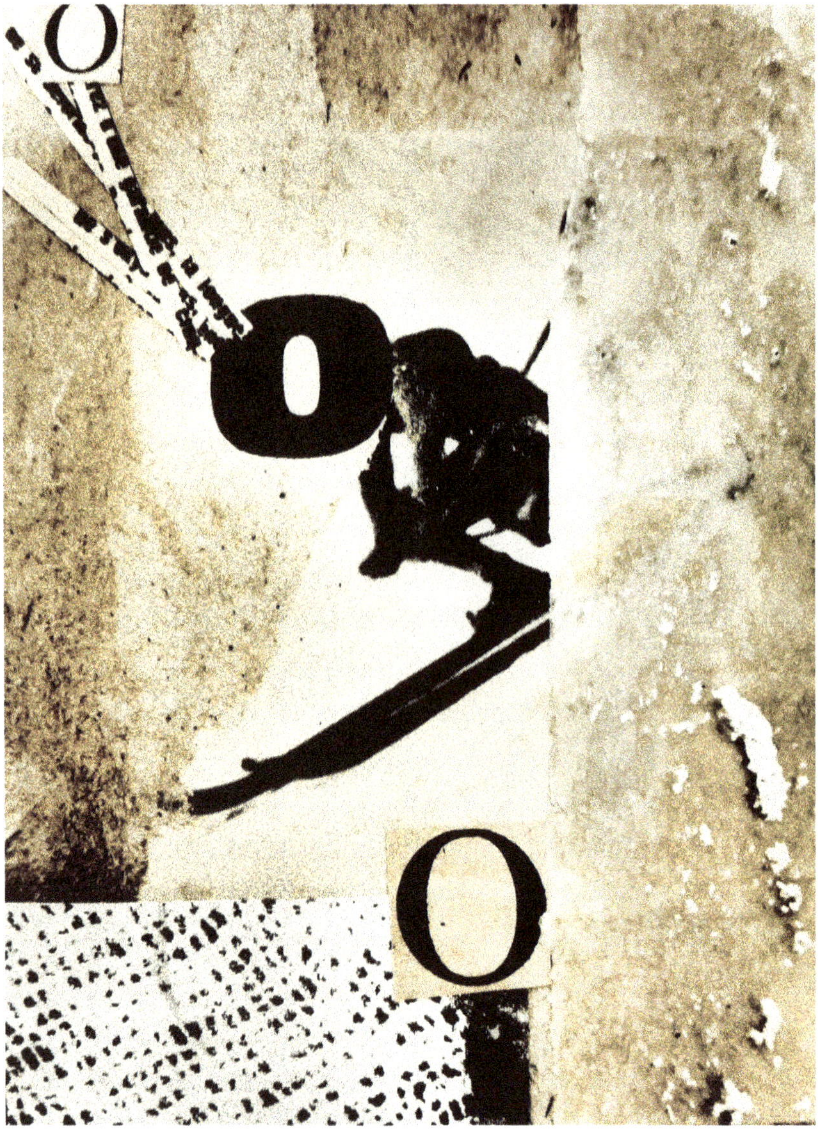

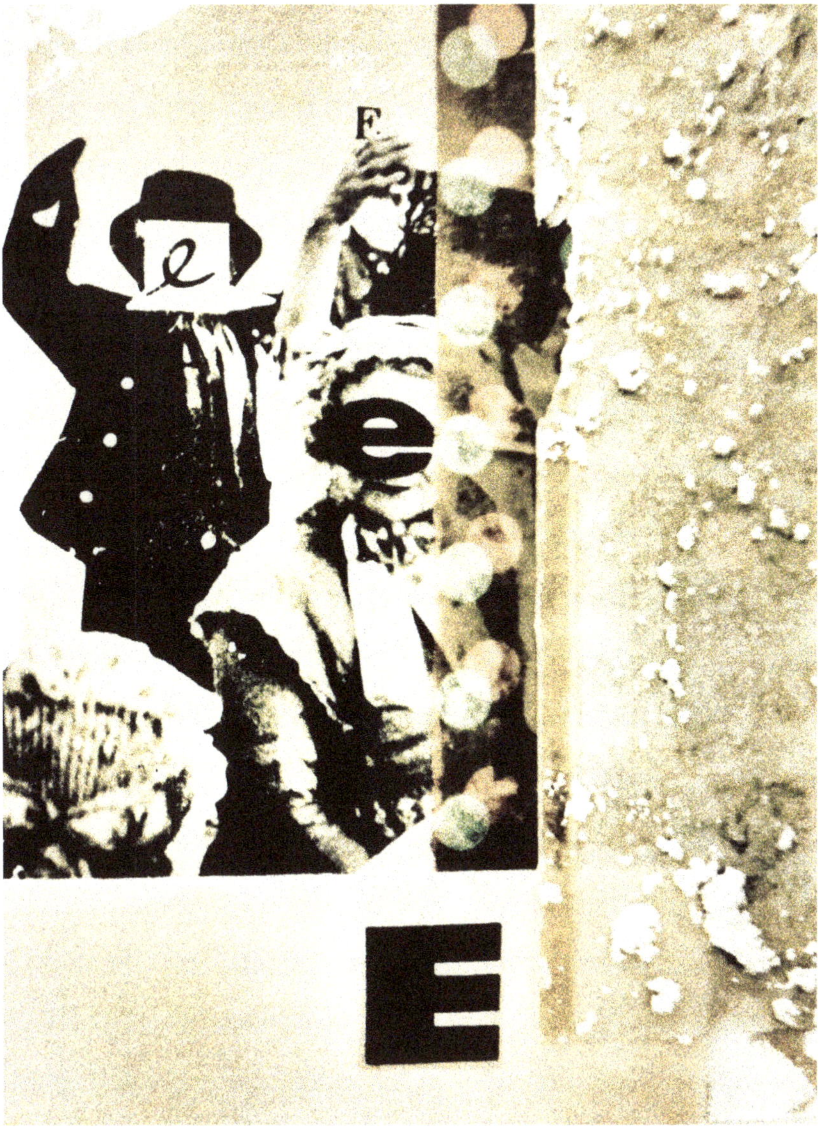
F
e
e
E

(untitled)

XYZ 0123456789

XYZ 0123456789

GHJKLMNPRSTVWXYZ 0123456789

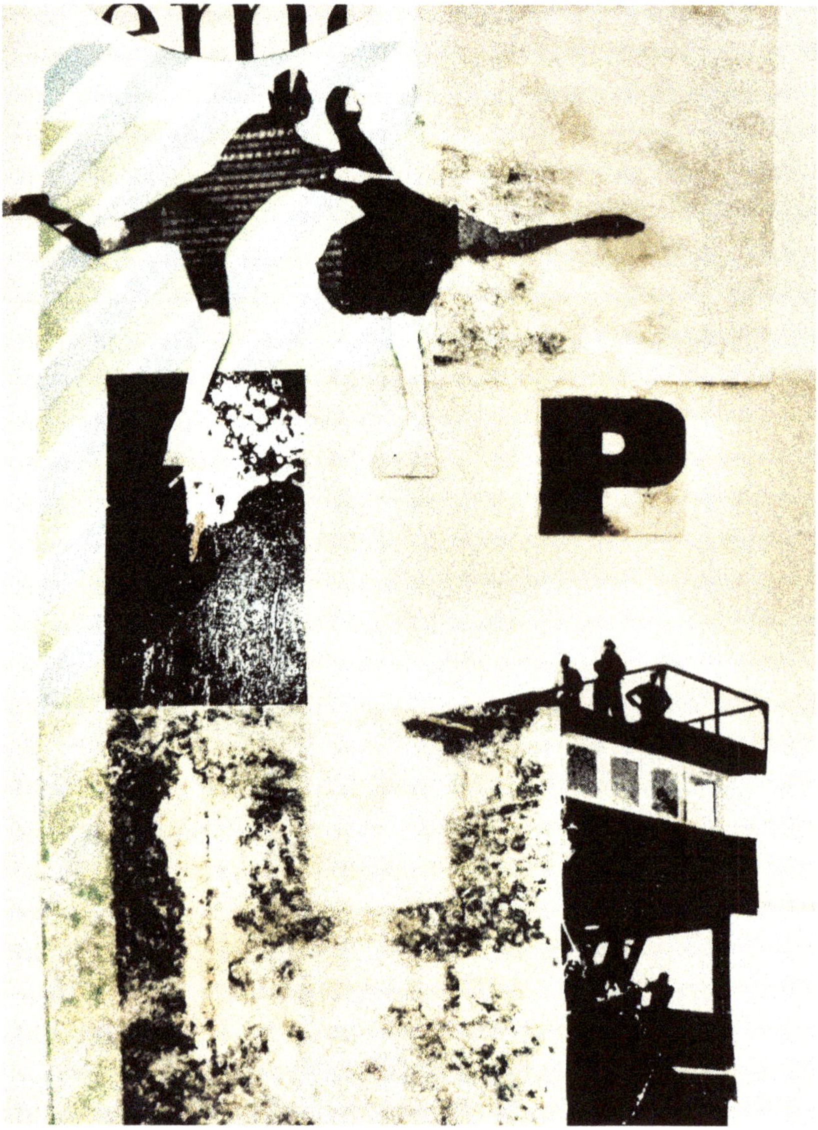
P

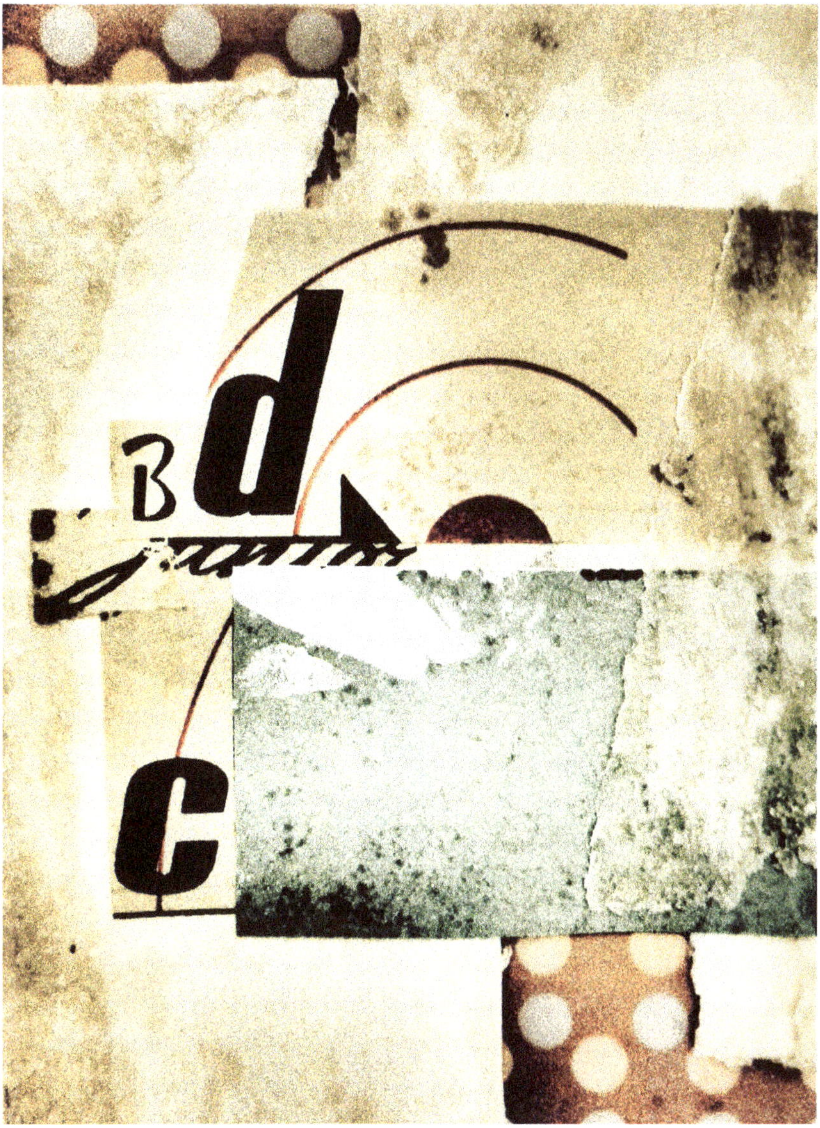
Bd
c

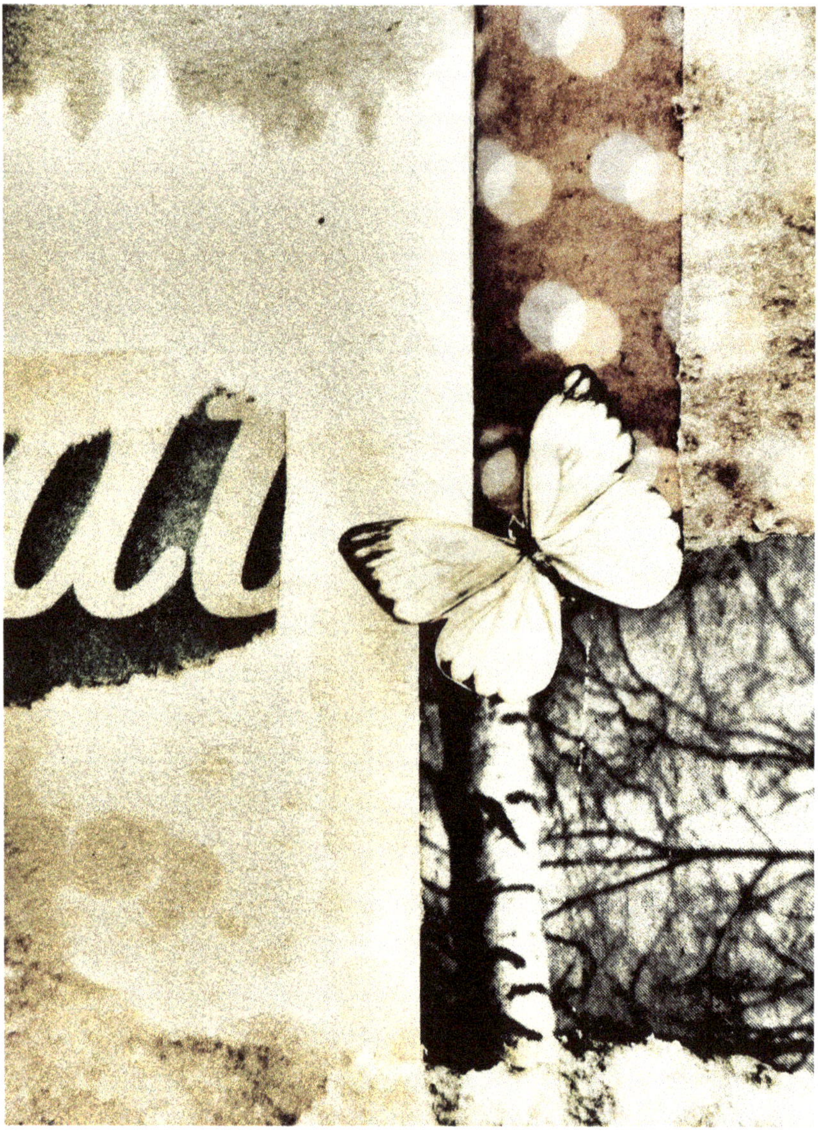

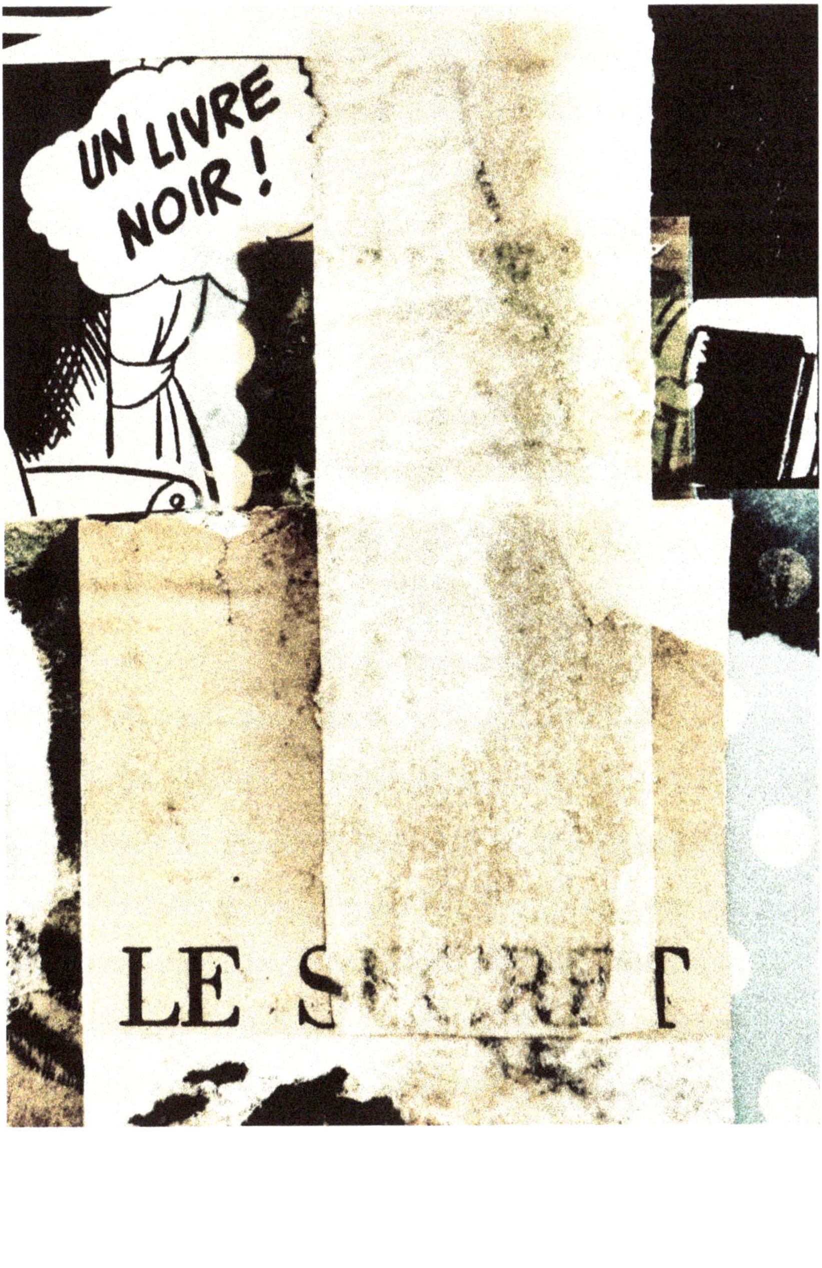
UN LIVRE NOIR !
LE

Burger Burglar

They were just hungry.
They didn't want diamonds, naturally, they didn't hope glittering money in their pocket.
They ran through the town and ordered chicken burgers at the counter of diner.
Burger with plenty of mayonnaise.

*

"I have always wanted to write a book that ended with the word 'mayonnaise.'"
— Richard Brautigan

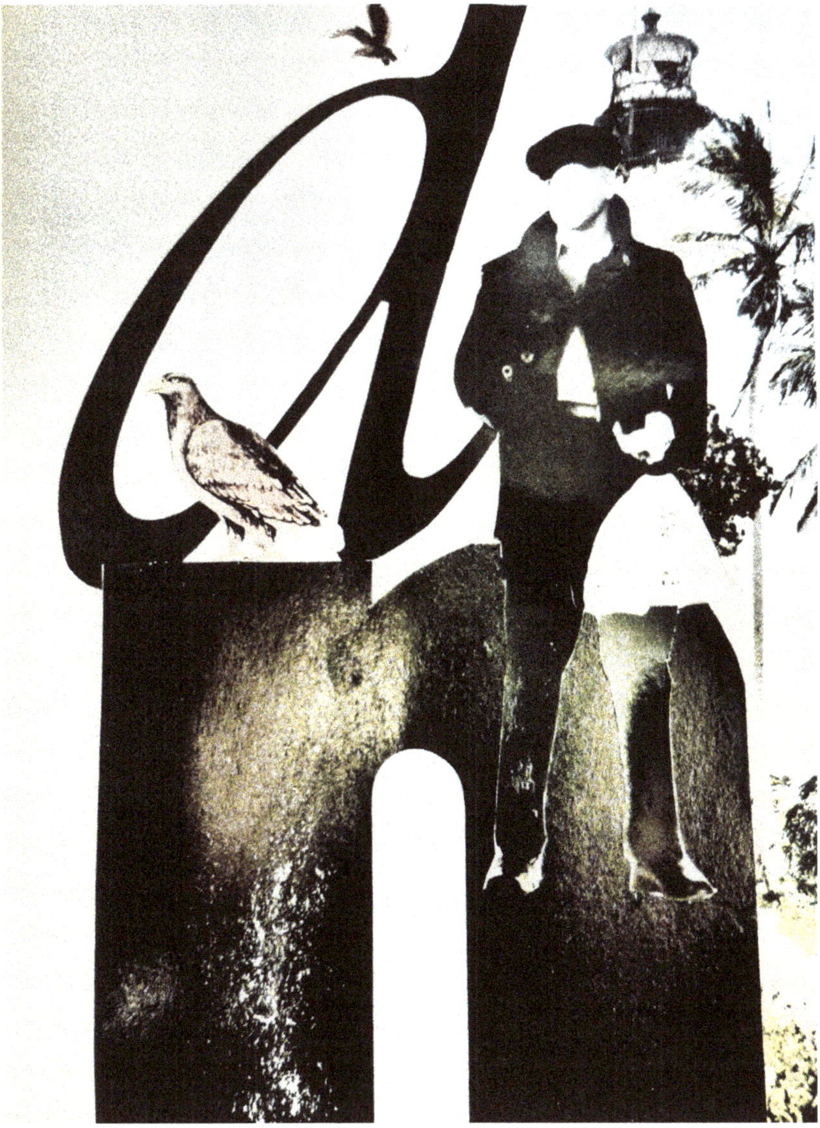

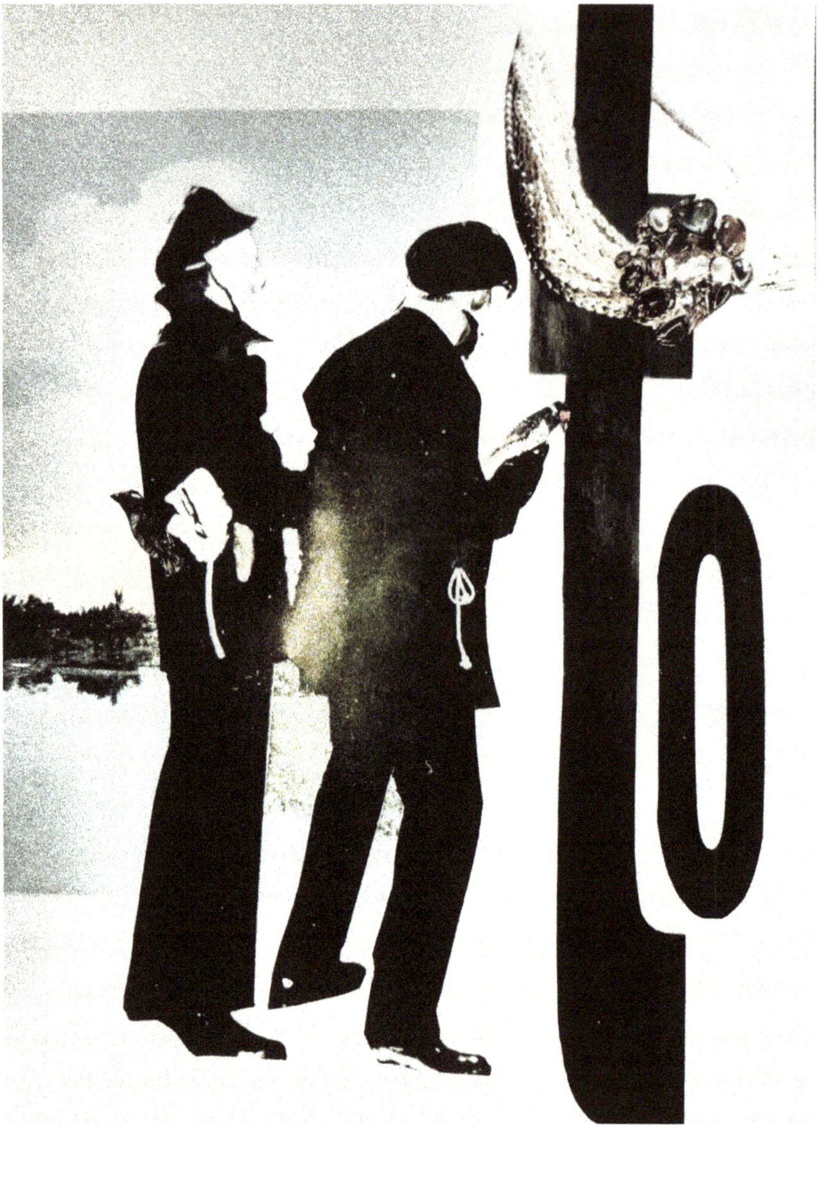

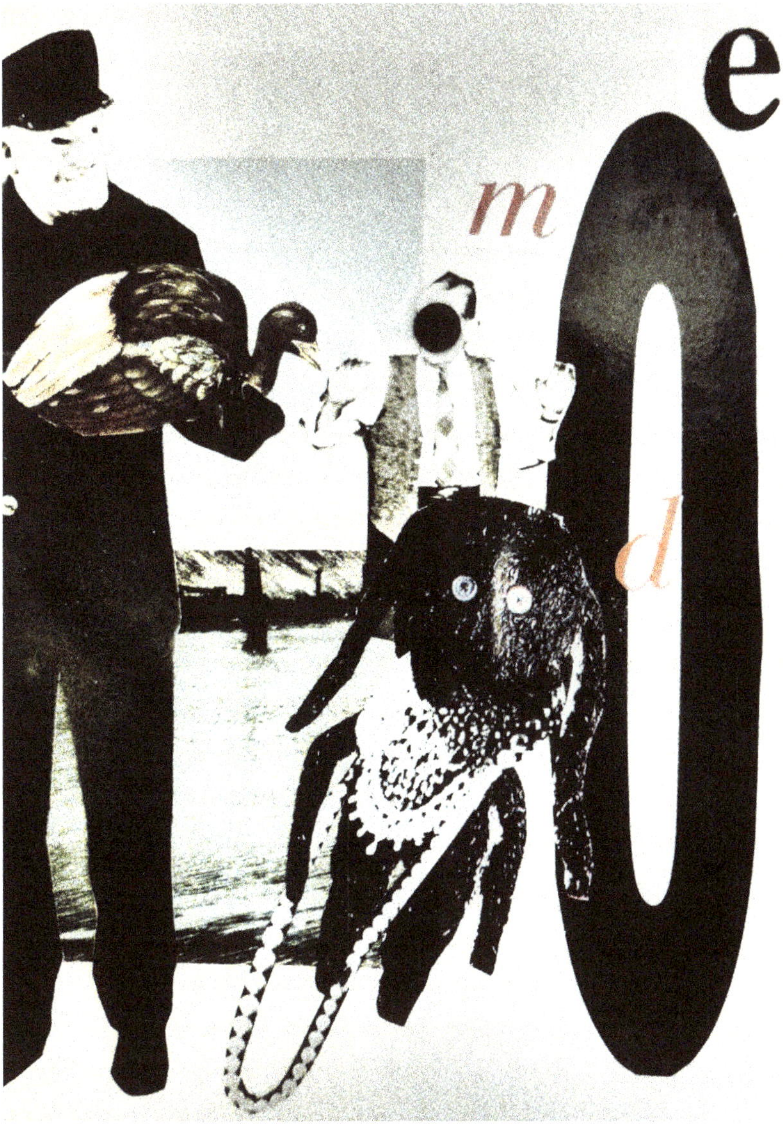
e
m
d
0

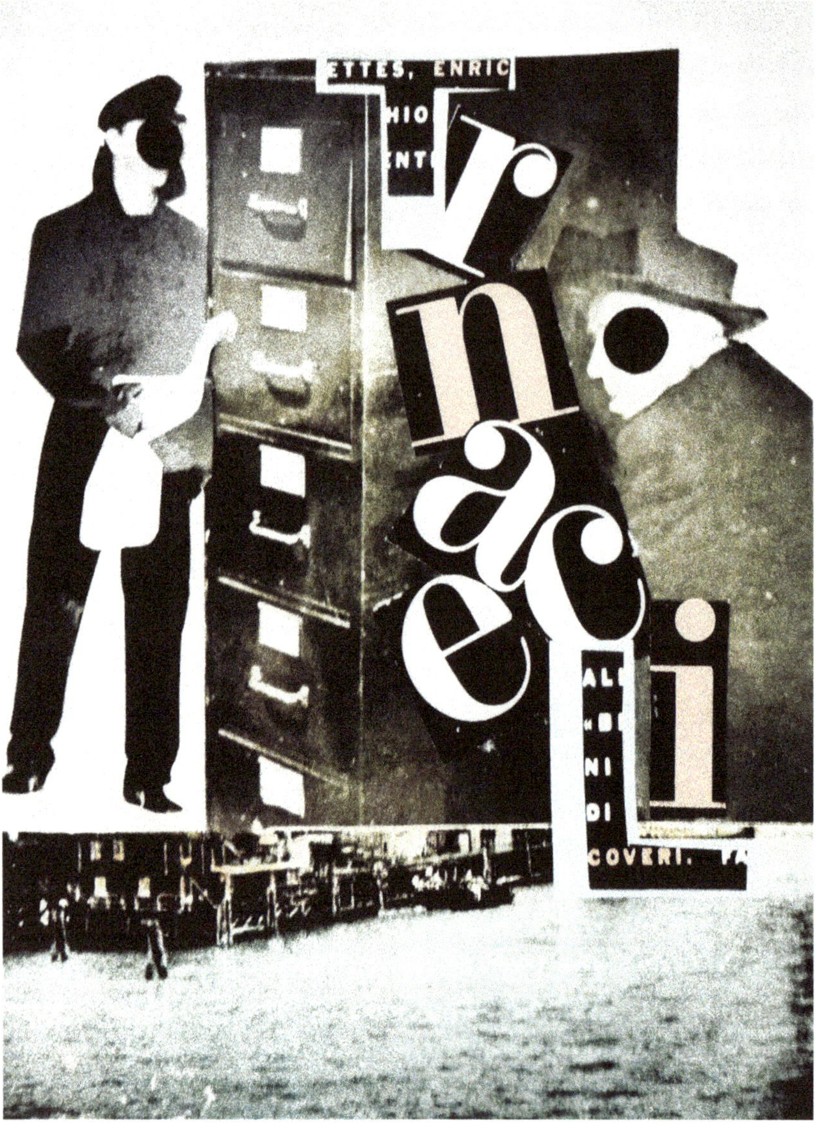
ETTES, ENRIC
COVERI.

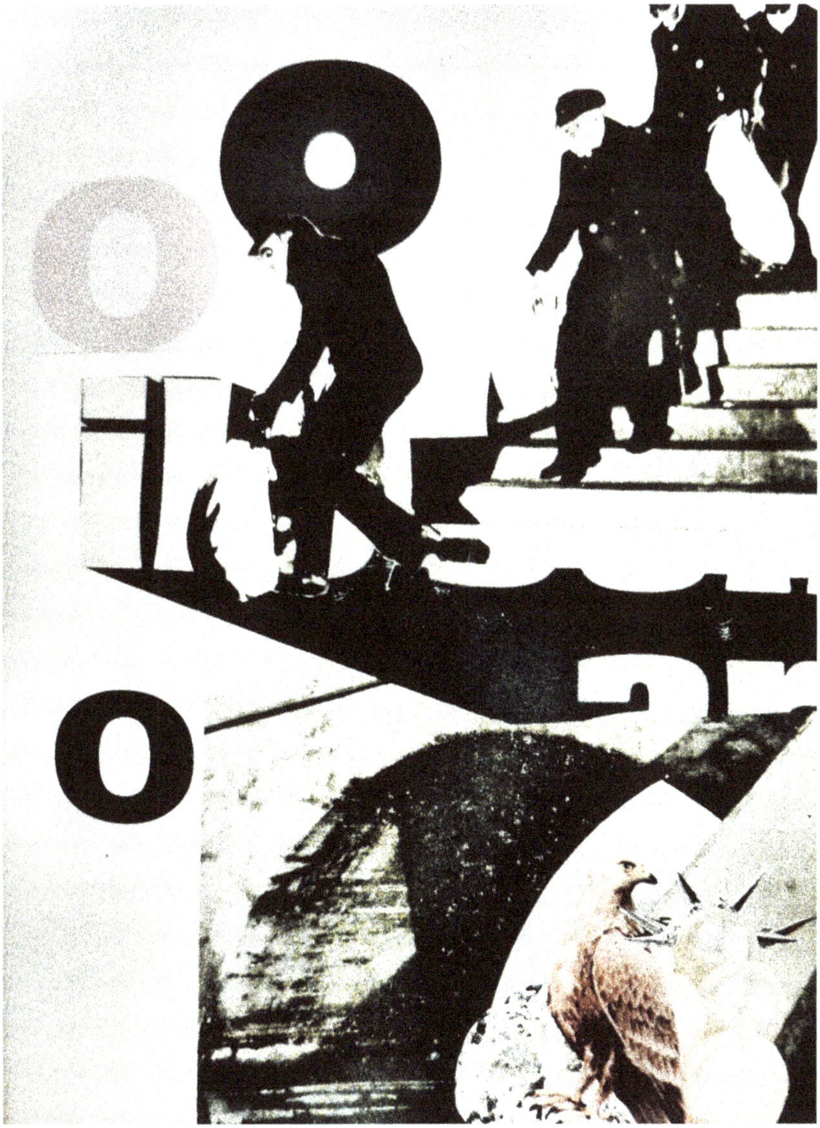

"Write a little every day, without hope, without despair."
– Karen Blixen

I make collages in a small notebook every night before I sleep.
I call it logbook.
They are diaries and also the place of creation for my art and
visual poetry. On my small desk that was used in an elementary
school which I bought at old furniture store, there are scrap
papers and the remains of past finished collages. I keep these in
(trash) boxes along with used stamps, pages from old magazines,
failed pieces, and so on.
My favourite material for logbook work is 'Ephemera' (garbage).

Like an otter swims through the culvert, I hold my logbook and
row a boat into the night. When I finished work, I look up at
the moon from my window. The moon also lights up my logbook.
I hear a voice and melody from the page.
An invisible story appears in the faint moonlight.
For me, visual poetry means invisible poetry.
I wonder if an otter could get to the river.
I wonder if he could get to the sea under the sun eventually.
I will continue rowing the boat in the night
and keep a logbook, looking for the invisible stories.

I am grateful to have been given this opportunity to
Paul Hawkins, publisher / editor of Hesterglock Press.

hiromi suzuki

publication history

(spreads)
Burning House Press (November, 2017)
*
Mare Vaporum
MOONCHILD MAGAZINE Issue 1 (October, 2017)
*
Post It
Obra/Artifact Issue 4 (October, 2017)
*
The seasons
Empty Mirror (November, 2017)
*
(untitled)
Utsanga.it magazine December Issue (December, 2017)
*
Burger Burglar
Empty Mirror (January, 2018)
*
with great thanks to all the editors,
Denise Enck of Empty Mirror,
Dhiyanah H and Miggy Angel of Burning House Press,
Francesco Aprile of Utsanga.it magazine,
Lucianna Chixaro Ramos of Obra/Artifact,
Nadia Gerassimenko of MOONCHILD MAGAZINE.
(alphabets)

biography

hiromi suzuki is an illustrator, poet, artist living in Tokyo, Japan. A contributor to the Japanese poetry magazine "gui" (run by members of the Japanese "VOU" group of poets, founded by the late Kitasono Katue). Author of Ms. cried, 77 poems by hiromi suzuki (kisaragi publishing, 2013 ISBN978-4-901850-42-1). My works are published internationally in Otoliths, BlazeVOX, Empty Mirror, Experiment-O, M58, DATABLEED, Black Market Re-View, Burning House Press, h&, BRAVE NEW WORD magazine, DODGING THE RAIN, Jazz Cigarette, TAPE HISS zine, The Arsonist Magazine, MOONCHILD MAGAZINE, Coldfront Magazine, 3:AM Magazine, NationalPoetryMonth.ca 2015 / 2017, and Poem Brut at Rich Mix London 2017, amongst other places.

web site: hiromisuzukimicrojournal.tumblr.com

0321